Education
for Employment :
Knowledge
for Action

Education for Employment: Knowledge for Action

Report of the
Task Force on
Education and Employment
National Academy
of Education

MARCH 1979

ACROPOLIS BOOKS LTD.
Colortone Building, 2400 17th St., N.W.
Washington, D.C. 20009

Printed in the United States of America by
COLORTONE PRESS, Creative Graphics Inc.
Washington, D.C. 20009

ACROPOLIS BOOKS
are distributed in

CANADA
by Carlton House, 91 Station Street,
Ajax, Ontario L1S 3H2

EUROPE AND THE BRITISH COMMONWEALTH
by Paul Maitland, 2/16 Mount Sion,
Tunbridge Wells, Kent TN1 1UF, England

JAPAN
by Atlantic Book Service, 23-17 Akabane Kita,
3-Chome Kita-Ku, Tokyo 15

PAKISTAN
by SASI Ltd., State Life Bldg #5
Zaibunnisa Street, GPO 779, Karachi 3

ELSEWHERE IN ASIA
by ICTO PTE Ltd., Wing On Life Bldg.,
150 Cecil Street, Singapore 1

Library of Congress Cataloging in Publication Data

Task Force on Education and Employment (U.S.)
  Education for employment.

  Bibliography: p.
  Includes index.
  1. Career education--United States. 2. Task
Force on Education and Employment (U.S.) 3. Educa-
tion--Economic aspects--United States. I. Kerr,
Clark, 1911   II. National Academy of Education.
III. Title.
LC1037.5.T37   1979   370.11'3   79-4029
ISBN 0-87491-243-1

Preface

Unprecedented numbers of young people have graduated from high school or reached the age of 18 over the past 10 years. Many of them are anxious about their chances in the labor market. Some of them question the value of additional schooling. Some adults who already have jobs must decide whether to upgrade their skills or get new ones. Others — mostly women with children — seek advice, support, and training to enter or reenter the work force.

The National Academy of Education asked us to review what is known about the relationship between education and employment and what is not known but should be. We were also asked to point out what the knowledge base means for the various sectors involved: employers, union leaders, teachers and other educators, students and parents, adults who seek to expand or refresh their knowledge and skills, government policy makers and the research community.

Among the questions we were asked to consider were: What advice should be offered to those contemplating additional schooling, a return to school, or entrance into a training program? What suggestions to school and college officials are warranted by demographic and labor market realities? How can public and private policy be improved to facilitate sensible decisions? What guidelines should be recommended to employers and unions?

We were asked to include in our report (1) an assessment of the extensiveness and usefulness of the existing knowledge base related to topics we have examined, and (2) an indication of areas where additional research and experimentation would be fruitful.

Early in our deliberations, we made two rather basic decisions that influence the tone and substance of our report. First, we felt that *education* should not be restricted to include only schools and colleges, and that *employment* should not be defined to include only work for pay. As Lawrence Cremin (1976, p. 22) reminds us: "family life does educate, religious life does educate, and organized work does educate; and . . . [each] is as intentional as the education of the school, however different in kind and quality." To be sure, much of what people learn contributes to paid employment, but it would be myopic to lose sight of other important objectives and values of education and our attention to non-paid service illustrates this more general point.[1] Second, in suggesting research, we restrict our attention to the knowledge needed for enlightened policy and individual decision making. Where the knowledge base appears adequate, we say so. Our recommendations for further research and experimentation[2] cover, therefore, basic knowledge deficits which, if remedied, would improve the quality of public and private decisions.

So that readers may know where each member of the Task Force stands, each recommendation has been given a priority rating in Appendix A.

One reason why another report on education and employment is needed at this time is that other recent and significant reports in this area — Wirtz's *Boundless Resource*, Ginzberg's *Manpower Connection*, and the Organisation for Economic Co-operation and Development's *Education and Working Life in Modern Society*, a report of the Secretary General's Ad Hoc Group on the Relations Between Education and Employment, chaired by Clark Kerr — do not contain a thorough assessment of knowledge and research needs. We have also arrived at somewhat different conclusions regarding the direction that some policies should take. Areas of disagreement between our report and the other three are discussed in Appendix B. Appendix C presents basic information about federal expenditures for education, training, and employment.

Now, as we issue our report, we wish to express our deep appreciation to John Shea, Senior Fellow of the Carnegie Council on Policy Studies in Higher Education, who provided staff assistance to our group. Sections 2 through 9 of our report are almost totally the result of his research and draftmanship. His efforts were absolutely essential to the completion of our effort and we considered him at all times a member of our group.

Members of the Task Force on Education and Employment[3]
Sponsored by the National Academy of Education

David W. Breneman
Senior Fellow
The Brookings Institution

Richard B. Freeman
Professor of Economics
Harvard University

William Gomberg
Professor of Management and
  Industrial Relations
The Wharton School,
  University of Pennsylvania

Ewald B. Nyquist[4]
Vice President for Academic Development
Pace University

Patricia Snider
Demographer
Human Resources Management Activity,
  General Motors Corporation

E. Belvin Williams
Senior Vice President
Educational Testing Service

Clark Kerr, Chairman of the Task Force
Chairperson
Carnegie Council on Policy Studies
  in Higher Education

---

[1]Alexis de Tocqueville (1832) wrote: "Americans of all ages, all conditions, and all dispositions, constantly form associations . . . . The Americans make associations to give entertainments, to found seminaries, to build inns, to construct churches, to diffuse books, to send missionaries to the antipodes: they found in this manner hospitals, prisons, and schools."

[2]In several instances, the term *model program* is more apt.

[3]Juanita Kreps served until her appointment as Secretary of Commerce.

[4]Commissioner of Education, State of New York, until July 1, 1977.

Acknowledgments

Our Task Force has had nearly two years to complete its work, funded by a grant from the Ford Foundation to the Academy for the general purpose of increasing the quality of public knowledge about educational thought and practice. We met four times, most recently in September 1977. At our meetings we called upon the knowledge and expertise of many people and would like to express our appreciation to them:

Paul Barton, National Manpower Institute
Michael Borus, The Ohio State University
Robert Campbell, The Ohio State University
John Dunlop, Harvard University
Eli Ginzberg, Beatrice Reubens, and Macia Freedman,
    Columbia University
Norman Gysbers, University of Missouri
Daniel Hamermesh, Michigan State University
Charles Holt and Ralph Smith, The Urban Institute
Brian Jones, American Institutes for Research
Vernon Jordan, Napoleon Johnson, and Carol
    Gibson, National Urban League
Jean Kessler, College Placement Council
Garth Mangum, University of Utah
Sidney Marland and Solomon Arbeiter, College
    Entrance Examination Board

Barbara McCandless, South Dakota Department
of Commerce and Consumer Affairs
David Mundel and Steve Chadima, Congressional
Budget Office
Dale Prediger, American College Testing Program
Corinne Reider, Robert Stump, and Ivan Charner,
National Institute of Education
Neil Rosenthal, U.S. Bureau of Labor Statistics
Barry Stern, Office of the Assistant Secretary
for Education, Department of Health, Education,
and Welfare
Ruth Shaeffer, The Conference Board
Benjamin Shimberg and Ronald Flaugher,
Educational Testing Service
Lewis Solmon, Higher Education Research Institute

We also wish to thank several members of the staff of
the Carnegie Council on Policy Studies in Higher Education. Margaret Gordon offered several helpful suggestions on an earlier draft of the report. Steve Archi-
bald provided valuable research assistance, and Sandra
Loris was responsible for typing the manuscript and
checking the bibliography.

Contents

Preface i
Acknowledgments v
1. Introduction: Where We Stand 1
2. Labor Market Realities: Present and Future 23
3. Problems of Youths in the Labor Market 48
4. Consequences of Schooling 63
5. Work-Education Programs 86
6. Career Guidance 106
7. Learning Needs of Adults 122
8. Employment and Training Programs 141
9. Occupational Licensure 161
10. Recommendations of the Task Force 168
   • To Educators 168
   • To Employers and Employee Organizations . . . 173
   • To Government Policy Makers 180
   • To Students, Parents, and the General Public . . 186
   • To the Research Community   191

Appendix A: Priority Ratings of Suggested Research,
            Experiments, and Policy
            Recommendations 199
Appendix B: Four Reports on Education and Work:
            Areas of Agreement and
            Disagreement 219

Appendix C: Trends in Federal Expenditures Related
           to Education and Employment 230
Biographical Sketches of Members
    of the Task Force 245
Bibliography 252
Index of Names 271

1.
Introduction: Where We Stand

Sensible public policy and private decision making in the area of education, work, and service depends, in part, on a better understanding of human behavior, of the needs and aspirations of people, of the work that needs to be done, and of the effectiveness of programs, services, and institutions. Also involved are notions of human decency, of the locus of responsibility, of societal well being, and of individual values. Our task has been to examine and report on the relationships between the acquisition and use of knowledge and skills — including attitudes and sensibilities — that contribute to the performance of useful tasks and the amount and quality of work activities (both paid and unpaid).

The topics we have selected for examination and our conclusions are informed by the following values:

- Each member of society should be able to choose from a reasonable set of opportunities: (1) curricular emphases in the schools; (2) college, work, or other postsecondary channels to adulthood; and (3) work, service, leisure, and continuing or recurrent education during one's potentially productive years.
- Education and training institutions should perform their functions effectively and efficiently.
- The amount and kind of education and training

1

should be responsive to the needs of the labor market as well as to individual desires and social needs.

• Schools and colleges should serve to strengthen the capacity and inclination of individuals to perform an array of important non-market-oriented work within families and the larger community.

The principal findings of the Task Force may be summarized in 14 observations, which fall into several general categories:

1. The composition of the labor force and the kinds of work people are paid to perform will change considerably over the next decade or so, but demographic trends suggest some easing in the years ahead of the serious employment problems faced by many young people.

Growth in the labor force — that is, entrants plus reentrants less attrition — will be considerably different over the next 15 years than it has been in the recent past. Between 1947 and 1976, the number of men 25 years of age or older in the civilian labor force rose by 8.7 million and the number of women 25 years of age or older increased by 11.6 million. The number of youths of both sexes under age 25 working or seeking work increased by 15.7 million, with much of the growth occurring over the past 15 years. From a slightly different perspective, adult men accounted for 59 percent of the total work force in 1947; in 1976, they represented only 46 percent. Youths of both sexes and adult women are now a majority of the labor force.

The "baby boom" of the 1940s will continue to be felt in the age structure of the work force. Men and women 25 to 44 years of age will account for practically all of the increase of nearly 20 million workers expected over

2

the next 10 years. The number of young people seeking work, which accelerated so rapidly from 1965 to 1974, will increase slightly between 1978 and 1980 and thereafter decline slightly. What this means, of course, is that youths entering the labor market in the 1980s will not face such stiff competition for jobs from their peers.

The most recent set of global projections of labor demand, prepared by the U.S. Bureau of Labor Statistics (BLS), covers the period from 1974 to 1985. Over this period, if the economy is basically healthy, some 58 million job openings are expected to materialize for new entrants (mostly young people) and reentrants (typically older women) to the civilian labor force.[1]

The occupational structure will continue to shift toward services as opposed to production activities. Of the 58 million openings for entrants and reentrants, 34 million are expected in white-collar work (professional, managerial, clerical, and sales), 11 million in service occupations, and 12.5 million in blue-collar categories. As many as seven of every ten openings will be to replace persons leaving the labor force by choice or because of death or retirement. The dominant role of attrition points to continuity in the kinds of work people will be paid to perform. If BLS projections are accurate, each of seven occupations will generate 100,000 or more openings per year. These seven occupations are: hospital attendants (nursing aides, orderlies, attendants), bookkeeping workers, secretaries and stenographers (the largest group), typists, retail trade salesworkers, building custodians, and waiters and waitresses. Only one of these — hospital attendants — is expected to employ 50 percent more people in 1985 than it employed in 1974; the other six are important because of their size to begin with and because turnover

3

is the dominant source of new openings. All told, these seven occupations are expected to account for nearly one-quarter of the 58 million job openings for entrants and reentrants. By comparison, 28 other rapid-growth occupations, each of which is expected to employ at least 50 percent more people in 1985 than in 1974, will account for only 6 percent of all openings.

We should point out that turnover varies considerably by occupation and industry. Furthermore, the BLS methodology, while helpful in describing the general pattern of change, is less useful for projecting developments in more detailed occupations. For instance, while the magnitude of openings for secretaries is broadly predictable, the employment of word processors is less so.

2. The economic value of a college degree has doubtless fallen for new graduates somewhat since the mid-1960s. Problems of adjustment in the supply of and demand for highly educated manpower[2] will continue, but the worst adjustment problems are probably over.

New college graduates seeking full-time work in the period since 1968 have experienced a lower rate of return on their investment in a college education than their counterparts who completed college earlier. This lower return is evidenced by a rather sharp decline in the earnings of college graduates 25 to 34 years of age in comparison with the earnings of high school graduates in this age group. However, the returns are still high by historical standards. Margaret Gordon (1977, pp. 2-3) points out, for example, that, 'The ratio of median income of male college graduates to that of male high school graduates declined somewhat between 1969 and 1975, but on the latter date was equal to its level of 1959

4

and well above the ratio for 1949. For women, the ratio was higher in 1975 than in 1969 and far above its 1949 level." The period from 1964 to 1969 was unusual in that a decrease took place in the ratio of college to high school graduates in the labor force. A very sharp turnaround, however, began in 1969. The number of persons in the work force with a high school education increased from only 38.4 to 39.8 million between 1969 and 1976. The number with four or more years of college shot up from 12.6 to 16.5 million. In part, this turnaround reflects the influence of the military draft in the earlier period and the lesser likelihood in recent years of college students going on to graduate school. Looking ahead through the 1980s, it is conceivable that as a smaller cohort of college graduates enters the labor market, the average rate of return on a college education for new graduates, which is still substantial, will increase somewhat in comparison with the corresponding cohort of the early and mid-1970s.

   3. Although individuals adjust quite quickly to changing opportunities, our ability to forecast changes in labor supply and demand, especially at a disaggregated level, is in need of improvement.

The problem of adjustments to recent demographic impacts, especially for burgeoning numbers of college graduates, reveals much about the resiliency of market forces and the behavior of young people seeking work, students continuing in school, and employers. Students respond more quickly than data-gathering agencies, but more slowly than would be socially optimal. Much of the decline in college-going rates has occurred among white males. In 1968, an estimated 55 percent of all high school graduates of that year entered college by fall. In

5

1976, the figure was 49 percent. Among men, the drop was from 63 to 47 percent (Young, 1977, p. 43). Outside of teaching, opportunities for women and minority men, especially in technical areas (engineering, business, etc.) have held up reasonably well. College-going rates have behaved accordingly. Between 1968 and 1976, the most recent year for which data are available, the percentage of women high school graduates entering college by fall was essentially unchanged (49 and 50 percent, respectively). Among young black high school graduates, the college-going rate rose slightly from 46 to 48 percent.

The earnings of new young workers at all levels — but especially among college graduates — have declined relative to older, more established workers. Some "bumping" of new high school graduates by the college-educated has occurred in middle-level (sales, clerical, craftworker) occupations. Outright unemployment among the college educated continues to be lower than among those with less education.

Without adjustments — other than those already implied in recent changes in college enrollment and graduation rates — projections of the Bureau of Labor Statistics indicate that demand conditions for those who will graduate over the next 10 years should be no worse, and probably will be better, than for youths who entered the job market since the late 1960s. Assuming a continuation in past trends in the percentage of college graduates in various occupations, some 12.1 million openings are forecast for persons receiving baccalaureate or higher degrees. This number is about 1 million lower than the number of college-educated persons likely to enter or reenter the work force. As one might expect, the outlook is brighter for some levels and

6

fields of study than others. The projected oversupply prior to adjustments is especially great for (1) Ph.D.-level manpower, especially in the liberal arts, because of the reduced need for college faculty; (2) baccalaureate holders, especially men, in nontechnical specialties; and (3) teachers in many areas because of steady or declining enrollments in the schools.

Sharp changes in government policy (for instance, response to the energy crisis, reduced spending on research and development) are difficult to forecast and result in violent pulsations in the labor market. But such changes — which are not informed by human resource considerations — are not the only reason forecasts go astray. Most projections are simply based on extrapolations of the past, with little or no attention to adjustment processes and to their implications until hindsight becomes possible — and even then agencies have been slow to detect and report on important turning points. The costs to individuals and society of a failure to develop greater sophistication in forecasting labor market developments, especially in fields and occupations where training is long, costly, and specialized, is great.

Adjustments to labor market conditions need not, of course, be the exclusive responsibility of young people. Colleges and universities, as "producers" of manpower as well as employers of faculty and staff, often contribute to imbalances by action or inertia. As we shall indicate in Section 10, employers — especially those with large numbers of employees, including colleges and universities — have an important role to play in speeding adjustment to changes in demographic and other realities affecting the labor supply.

4. While broad trends are generally predictable

7

and favorable, there are several groups of persons who face special problems in the job market: inner-city youths (especially hispanic and black) not in school and without work; women reentering the work force; and older persons nearing retirement or with special employment needs stemming from disability or displacement.

Demographics are important but somewhat less salient in the case of these special groups. Inadequate schooling and the absence of nearby employment opportunities are serious problems for disadvantaged youths. Extremely high unemployment rates and relatively low labor force participation rates are symptomatic of the enormous difficulties facing large numbers of youths in large, urban areas. Women — especially those with few skills and little work experience and who are divorced, widowed, or separated — need support, education, and training opportunities, help in finding jobs, child care, and other assistance. Finally, many older men and women face special problems in adapting to second careers upon nearing retirement or in the event of disability or work obsolescence.

At least since Cairnes (1874), many economists, including Dunlop (1957) and Kerr (1954), and extending to Doeringer and Piore (1971) and others, have been concerned about boundary lines around particular labor markets and difficulties many "outsiders" face in gaining access to preferred employment at decent wages, in secure jobs, offering the potential to learn and advance along internal promotion ladders. We fear that large numbers of young people — especially minority youths with less than a high school education — will have great difficulty moving from relatively un-

8

structured, often rather casual "youth jobs" to more secure career positions. Certainly, the sheer size of the present youth cohort points to the probability that many young people will find the process of work establishment a long and painful one.

While barriers between unstructured and structured employment are not impenetrable, large numbers of young people — especially women and minorities with little education — will doubtless remain mired in a secondary labor market. What is needed to ease this problem is a series of improvements in schooling, counseling, and especially job placement and encouragement to employers to develop more good jobs and to invest in those members of the work force who are now "outsiders" to preferred employment.

5. Additional years of schooling, for most people, have real and long-lasting effects on their economic well being and on several noneconomic aspects of their lives.

Research consistently demonstrates a positive relationship between highest year of school completed and success in the labor market, as measured by occupational status, earnings, and employment stability — not for each individual, but on the average. Native ability, what happens at home and in one's neighborhood, and other factors — including experiences in school — doubtless influence how much education people obtain, but plenty of room is left for personal effort, aspirations, and other influences. Highest year of school completed, while affected by school achievements in the early grades, is not an accurate mirror of ability differences apart from schooling.

Recent work by Jencks and his associates (1972), Berg (1971), and Bird (1975) call attention to what has long

9

been known — namely, that additional years of schooling do not assure success at work and that not everyone is handicapped by a lack of formal education. There is considerable overlap in the annual earnings distributions of white male high school graduates versus college graduates. Self-made millionaires do exist. A few people with doctorates drive taxicabs, and it should come as no surprise that they are about as productive in such jobs as others. It is a fallacy however, for two reasons, to conclude that schooling makes no difference. First, additional years of schooling increase the probabilities of being selected for better, more productive jobs. Second, the jobs people obtain surely reflect some real differences in ability, much of which, we believe, is a consequence of the schooling process. While few studies have been able to control statistically for underlying differences in ability, those which have suggest that anywhere from 0 to 40 percent of the relationship between highest years of school completed and later labor market attainments is a reflection of innate ability differences.

Arrow (1973), among others, has argued that educational attainment serves as a filter or screen, signaling latent productive potential. Consider the hiring of college graduates. Large employers (and many small ones) hire college graduates for two reasons: First, in fields such as engineering, law, and accounting, graduates have specialized skills needed by companies. Second, large employers especially want talented people who have demonstrated a capacity to learn and who can see relationships, apply knowledge from one area to another, make decisions, synthesize information, and communicate effectively. College raises the probability of, but does not ensure, such abilities. The "screening hypothesis" implies that the college degree simply indicates something about an individual's preexisting productivity — as the Good Housekeeping Seal of Approval does with products. If true, this could mean that total social "returns" on a college education per se are less than the benefits received by those individuals who persevere in the system until labeled "college graduates." The fact that credentials are important does not necessarily imply that the relationship between educational attainment and earnings is an artificial one. Recently, Layard and Psacharopoulos (1974, p. 985), on the basis of an examination of the literature on the "screening hypothesis," concluded:

> Three predictions in the spirit of the hypothesis are not in fact borne out. First, rates of return to uncompleted courses (dropouts) are as high as to completed courses. Second, standardized educational differentials rise with age, although employers have better information about older employees' abilities. Third, if screening is the main function of education, it could be done more cheaply by simpler testing procedures. Yet these are not used widely despite the profits that could, according to the hypothesis, be made by those developing them.

Even though more young people with high school diplomas and college degrees have chosen (or have only been able to find) work in occupations which in the past have not employed large numbers of people with as much education, evidence points to beneficial effects of schooling outside the employment relationship. A number of studies reveal a positive association between years of school completed and physical condition, effective parenting, contribution through voluntary service, and adaptation to external forces and new

11

opportunities. At the same time, measured job satisfaction is largely unrelated to educational attainments, probably because better-educated persons expect more. Two recent studies reveal, interestingly enough, that college graduates with low incomes are about as satisfied as those with high. Among persons with less education, income bears a much stronger relationship to satisfaction. One possible explanation is that education adds to the capacity of people to derive satisfaction outside the employment relationship.

6. Recent declines in test scores are attributable, in part, to greater equality of opportunity in access to higher education. But a change in the composition of test takers is only one factor, and questions have arisen as to curriculum content, seriousness of purpose, and the way students spend their time, both in and outside of school. The implications of declining test scores for worklife are not entirely clear.

Scores on standardized tests have declined since the early 1960s above grade 5. Wiley and Harnischfeger (1976) also note that test score declines have been especially noticeable among college-bound women and in more complex verbal areas of comprehension and interpretation.[3] In 1977, an Advisory Panel on the Scholastic Aptitude Test Score Decline, chaired by Willard Wirtz, reported its findings. SAT scores have declined since 1963. In the 1960s, about two-thirds to three-fourths of the drop can be attributed to change in the composition of test takers. Proportionately more women, who score lower than men in mathematics, took the test. Proportionately more youngsters from low income and minority groups could be found among the test takers.

Between 1970 and the present, however, only one-fifth to one-third of the decline stems from a change in the population taking the SAT. The Wirtz Panel ruled out change in test items as a cause of the decline, but drew attention to other possibilities: a reduced emphasis in school and home on writing; reduced homework; turmoil stemming from the Vietnam and Watergate periods; television; family structure and interaction; and changes in the curriculum.

It is heartening, in terms of SAT scores, that there is no evidence that a modest mixing of schooling and paid work reduces test scores. On the contrary, test takers reporting 1 to 15 hours of work per week had average test scores above those of students who did not work at all or who worked more than 15 hours per week (Wirtz and others, 1977, p. 41). Wiley and Harnischfeger feel that a portion of the decline found in a variety of tests may stem from students spending less time in school and taking fewer academic courses. Contrary to popular belief, students may be spending less time on school work now than 20 or 30 years ago. More time is taken for parent conferences, and changes have occurred in the course and program options students exercise. Specialty courses (for example ecology and science fiction) have to some extent replaced more traditional academic courses. This raises the question of whether standardized tests are measuring as well as in the past what students are asked to learn. The answer is not completely clear. SAT scores are more strongly corre-lated with grades than in the past and still predict very well successful completion of the freshman year of college. At the same time, the relevance of test score declines for "life beyond school" is less clear. Surely, for most jobs, basic competency in verbal and mathematical areas is very important, especially for movement to higher rungs on promotion ladders.

7. Research on the effects of schooling indicates that doubling school resources does not double learning. Nevertheless, more schooling helps, and extreme pessimism as to the effects of schooling on later achievements is unfounded.

Research by Coleman and his associates (1966) and by Jencks and others (1972) sharply questions the influence of resources devoted to schooling on educational and labor market outcomes. However, more recent research points to the importance of time spent on school work, a variable all but ignored by Coleman and his colleagues. The importance of time actually spent in and out of school studying what a curriculum offers can be seen in the rather consistent, positive relationship between number of years of school completed and labor market and other achievements. Most research on "school effects" has ignored this point. The question generally posed has been whether, controlling for highest year of school completed, existing variation in school resources has made much difference. This ignores the time question as well as the effects of early schooling on highest year of school completed. Extreme pessimism based on Coleman's and Jencks' reports is unfounded on other grounds as well. Most research on schooling effects has used such variables as district-wide expenditures per pupil and library books per pupil. Such measures hide differences between schools and classrooms and say nothing about whether resources are used in instruction. It must surely make a difference whether (and how often) books are read. One thing large-scale surveys do reveal, however, is that crude measures of the environment outside the school (for example, highest year of school completed by father and mother) correlate strongly with both the amount of schooling and later attainments. Little is known, however, about the interactive effects of schooling and home life, but some have suggested that parent involvement in Head Start and similar programs through the early elementary years may be a factor in the absence of declining test scores in the early grades.

8. Major curricular options in the high school respond to individual differences in aptitudes and interests by widening choices. Vocational courses tend to be psychologically congenial for many youths, and have a modest positive impact on the earnings of young women who do not go on to college.

Most high school students either like or feel neutral about practical subject matter courses: business and clerical, agricultural, and skilled manual blue-collar work. Negative feelings are common in academic areas. There are, however, important differences by sex and race. Most young men like vocational or commercial courses; many rate them as favorites, especially vocational and general students. Young black men are somewhat less favorably inclined toward vocational courses than their white peers and rate course work in the humanities more positively. Most young women like courses in occupational areas.

Students in the three major curriculum categories — academic, vocational, and general — differ from one another in several ways. College preparatory students (about 40 percent of the total) stand out from their peers on measures of mental ability and socioeconomic background. Among the remainder, girls in vocational

15

studies rank higher than their general peers, while boys in vocational areas rank lower. Curriculum choice (or assignment) coincides with educational aspirations, which are, on the whole, high among secondary school students. Those who remain in a college curriculum from one year to the next raise their already high aspirations. Boys who stay in a vocational program two years in a row lower theirs. The few students who shift generally feel better about their educational experience. It is not clear, however, whether moving to a vocational program keeps youngsters in school. For some it may; for others it does not seem to. Compared with the general program student, students in vocational areas complete fewer years of school, with most of the difference manifest in rates of college attendance.

Among youths who leave school at high school graduation, having been in a vocational program rather than a general program makes little difference for the labor market success of young men, but is helpful for young women. On the whole, youths in this group who were in a vocational program are somewhat more likely than others to feel their education has met their needs. Some evidence indicates that vocational male graduates profit more from further training after high school than their peers in other curricula, but large portions from all three curriculum categories acquire experience and training in a variety of postsecondary alternatives to college: business colleges and technical institutes, company programs, and military service and apprenticeships.

9. Work-education programs vary enormously in purpose, organization, and clientele served. This variation may explain the uncertain consequences of such programs in general. Program quality and choice of work

16

assignment seem to be important determinants of the longer-term consequences of having participated in a work-education program.

Increased numbers of students, both in high school and college, are combining schooling with paid (and unpaid) work. Some portion of the trend is attributable to growth since the early 1960s of work-study, cooperative education, and other work experience programs such as the Neighborhood Youth Corps. Students, employers, and parents generally view such programs positively because, by providing income, they open opportunity for further schooling and economic independence at an earlier age.

Advocates of work-education programs emphasize career exploration, discovery of one's aptitudes and interests, feelings of contribution, and acquisition of useful skills. At the same time, sponsored work in high schools — especially for low-income, disadvantaged youngsters — may well reduce attainments in school. With respect to longer-term consequences, the average effects are modest at best. Several studies (summarized in Section 5) indicate that the quality of jobs, linkages to instructional activities, and choice of work make a positive contribution to the learning values of early work experiences. While anecdotal evidence is frequently cited, we have found no careful studies demonstrating that work-education programs are especially beneficial to women and minority men. They probably are, but evidence one way or the other is lacking.

10. The services of paid guidance personnel constitute a small but important part of a larger set of formal and informal influences which guide young people (and adults) as they make

career development decisions at many points in their lives.

Numerous studies reveal that when it comes to educational and occupational decisions, parents and friends, books, and often teachers are a preferred source of information and advice compared with guidance counselors. Work experience, avocational activities, and television are also important channels of influence. Guidance counselors are, however, important in several areas, including course scheduling, providing information about careers, financial aid, and choice of college.

11. Advances in career development theory, expanded options, and certain technological developments point to the desirability of comprehensive systems of career guidance that encourage maximum self-direction.

Many students and adults out of school seek fair, unbiased information about themselves and their opportunities; some, however, question the utility of help provided by school personnel. School guidance counselors usually know more about colleges than they do about the labor market and noncollegiate options, and many are overburdened with routine administrative chores. However, advances in career development theory — including a recognition of differences in motivation and need and the information requirements implied by expanding options in the postsecondary years — have led to a rethinking of the functions of guidance personnel. Increasingly, comprehensive systems are being developed — using the curriculum from the elementary grades onward, print and nonprint (that is, computer) materials on occupational and educational options, career centers, work-experience programs, and other resources — to assist people in making choices.

18

Many guidance counselors see their role as one of helping people learn about and apply career decision-making skills: examining interests aptitudes, and other characteristics of self; clarifying values; setting goals; searching for information and so forth. Guidance personnel are increasingly involved in the design and direction of guidance systems, working with teachers, parents, community resource people, and the like. Interest inventories also continue to be an important tool of guidance personnel, although they are increasingly viewed as devices to prompt exploration of further options rather than as prescriptions of what a person should do.

12. There is probably a need for more career development services and improvement of those which exist, yet empirical evidence on the comparative utility of alternative guidance services is lacking.

The influence of some guidance activities can be assessed: for example, whether career awareness activities lead to greater occupational information. The development of job-seeking skills such as letters of application and job interview skills can also be evaluated. Complex and longer-term outcomes (for example, motivation, acquisition of basic skills, and job satisfaction), however, are more difficult to determine and have been investigated only rarely.

13. Increasing numbers of adults — including persons nearing retirement — are participating in adult, recurrent, or lifelong education. Issues such as benefits and costs, individual and social needs, and public finance are just beginning to be addressed.

Estimates of the nature and extent of 'lifelong learning" vary enormously and depend on how such activities are measured. One estimate is that 13 million Americans above the age of 16 participated in courses on a part-time basis in 1969; a comparable measure indicates that the number rose to 17 million by 1975. Sponsors range from well-established public institutions to individual tutors and community-based organizations such as the Red Cross. About half the learning was reported to be for vocational or occupational purposes. Very little was social/recreational. Methods of finance vary, with individuals and employers meeting a large share of reported costs.

Increasing productivity, better health and longer lives, and the changing age composition of the population suggest that adult learning will continue to grow at least moderately in the years ahead. Although solid evidence is sparse, recurrent education is sometimes considered a partial solution to social problems such as the health and well-being of senior citizens and easier access of minorities and women to preferred jobs.

Several federal initiatives provide prototype models of lifelong education for specific purposes and clientele: Adult Basic Education (for literacy); Vocational Rehabilitation, the GI Bill, and federal employment and training programs to meet the personal development and job needs of clientele who face serious obstacles in the labor market. More diverse community service projects illustrate other ways publicly supported education and training can be of service to adults. A great deal of adult learning takes place in both the private and public sectors, where tuition aid, sabbaticals for teachers, and other programs exist.

At least three approaches to additional public financing of life-long learning are under consideration:

20

tax credits, modification in student financial aid programs, and categorical support for programs or clients. Each can be expected to vary in impact and cost. Relatively little is known about the implications of tuition assistance and other forms of public support in either real or financial terms. Issues of equity, purpose, and benefits are involved in each.

14. A careful, wide-range review is needed of the effectiveness and impact of federal programs related to education, work, and service.

Since the early 1960s, many new programs and a great deal of money have been directed toward improving the relationship between education and employment. Certain general trends are evident — toward greater state and local responsibility for instruction and provision of services, toward heavier emphasis on income transfers and public service jobs (see Appendix C). What is now needed is a careful evaluation of the entire array of programs to determine what changes are likely to make the most sense as we look ahead to the year 2000.

We have concluded, in general, that an all-out effort is needed to acquire more knowledge and stimulate more action in eight specific areas:

1. Developing basic skills;

2. Improving the quality of work-education programs by improving teaching, involving parents and greater use of performance examinations to monitor progress, and by including opportunities for students to leave school temporarily for work or service;

3. Developing more comprehensive and systematic guidance and counseling services for youths and adults;

4. Involving parents, everyday citizens, and community leaders in the work of schools, and fostering

21

productive relationships between the worlds of work and formal education;

5. Finding ways to finance and encourage recurrent education in areas of substantial benefit to individuals and to the larger society;

6. Focusing greater attention on the education and employment needs of groups all too often treated as "outsiders" — for example, out-of-school urban youths with little education or work experience;

7. Determination of which government programs are working well, which are not, and what can be done at federal, state, and local levels to improve the relationship between education and employment; and

8. Identification of the probable nature of human resource, employment, and educational problems likely to emerge in the 1980s and 1990s.

---

[1]To be precise, this number refers not to jobs as such but to individuals who may be expected to be at work. The BLS statistics ignore multiple job holding, and part-time jobs and short work weeks open up numerous possibilities for holding more than one job: two parents each working part time, and so forth.

[2]We are aware of the sexist implication of the term *manpower*. We use the term, nevertheless, because other terms, such as *labor supply* and *human resources*, are less apt in referring to the development through time of the power of individuals to contribute to production.

[3]The authors' findings are based on trends on a wide variety of tests, including the Scholastic Aptitude Test (grades 11 and 12); the American College Testing Program (grades 11 and 12); the Minnesota Scholastic Aptitude Test (grade 11); the Iowa Test of Educational Development, given only in Iowa (grades 9 through 12); the Iowa Tests of Basic Skills, given only in Iowa (grades 5 through 8); the Comprehensive Test of Basic Skills (grades 6 through 10); and the National Assessment of Educational Progress (science and writing, ages 13 and 17).

2.
Labor Market Realities:
Present and Future

Enormous changes have occurred over the past 30 years in the composition of the labor force. Especially dramatic have been increases in the numbers of young people and adult women.[1] In this section, three topics are examined: (1) the probable future demand for labor services, (2) the likely available supply, and (3) the accuracy and usefulness of manpower forecasts.

Before going on, we should clarify the terms *shortage* and *surplus*. The traditional meaning of these terms is that at existing rates of pay, vacancies exist and cannot be filled (shortage) or there are more job seekers than jobs offered (surplus). A more precise meaning, from a dynamic multi-year perspective is that the private rate of return on an investment in a college education is such that it encourages a larger (or smaller) fraction of young people to attend college. These technical terms are used, however, in less precise ways. In the market for physicians, some argue that there is a shortage, based either on extremely high salaries associated with restrictions on supply or a target ratio of physicians to people. In other markets, such as private household workers, a shortage may mean that some employers cannot find workers at prices paid in the recent past. Figure 2.1 illustrates the household worker market. Many people withdrew from this market between 1940 and 1970 because of changing attitudes, better employment opportunities, and similar factors. Moreover, employer decisions are responsive to changes in price (wages). Hence, while household workers earn more, significantly fewer are employed: between 1940 and 1970, the number of employed household maids declined from 2.4 million to 1.0 million (Wool, 1976).

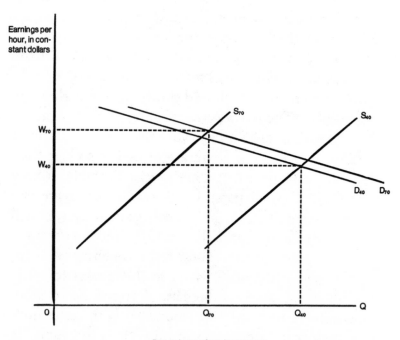

Figure 2.1
Market for Private Household Workers

Person hours of service per year

Supply: The Underlying Demographics

The age composition of the work force will change dramatically in the years ahead as the "baby boom" generation progresses through the age structure of the population. Between 1960 and 1975, youths 16 to 24 years of age in the labor force increased by nearly 11 million — nearly half the total expansion in the civilian labor force of 23 million persons. Between 1975 and 1990, however, while the economically active population is expected to expand by approximately 21 million, adult workers will account for all but 2 percent of the growth. Indeed, the number of youths in the labor force is expected to decline throughout the 1980s, following a moderate expansion from 22.0 million in 1976 to 24.3 million in 1980. Thereafter, the projected numbers are 23.1 million in 1985 and 21.0 in 1990 (Fullerton and Flaim, 1976, p. 9). The decline, however, will not be uniform by race. Between 1975 and 1985, for example, Labor Department projections suggest that the number of white 16- to 24-year-olds in the civilian labor force will remain essentially unchanged, while the number of minorities will increase by over one-half million, or by nearly one-fifth. The reason: somewhat higher birth rates among blacks than whites (see U.S. President, 1977, p. 258).

According to projections of the U.S. Bureau of Labor Statistics (BLS), the number of adult women at work will increase, but at a slower pace than the trend of the past 30 years. In 1947, 87 percent of all men 16 and older were working or looking for work compared with 32 percent of the women. In 1976, the rates were 78 and 47 percent, respectively. A rise in the number of adult women workers of 11.6 million accounted for about one-third of the total growth in the work force of 36.0 million.

In 1947, adult men represented 59 percent of the civilian labor force. In the years since, youths of both sexes and adult women have increased their collective share of the civilian labor force from 41 to 54 percent. While there were 8.7 million more adult male workers in 1976 than in 1947, the increase accounted for only 24 percent of the total growth. Increased numbers of youths (15.7 million more) and of adult women (11.6 million) clearly dominated the change.

In the years from 1975 to 1990, if BLS projections are correct, adult women will represent over half (54 percent) of total growth in the civilian labor force of 21.2 million. Since the number of youth workers is likely to decline by 1990 (because of reduced fertility subsequent to 1961), adult males will represent nearly the same percentage of total growth in the work force as adult females.[2]

Expected Demand: An Overview

Assuming a healthy economy, total civilian employment is expected to grow by 20 percent between 1974 and 1985, from 86 to 103 million (Carey, 1976). These BLS projections indicate that 58 million job openings will arise over the period on two accounts: (1) 70 percent from retirements and other withdrawals from the labor force, and (2) 30 percent from growth in total employment. Employment opportunity in various occupations will depend on several factors, including increases in output, changes in productivity and in methods of production within various sectors or industries, and movement out of the labor force entirely.[3] As nonhousehold service industries expand, for example, growth will occur in occupations concentrated in that sector — allied health, law enforcement and the like. Ignoring occupational mobility, over half of projected openings are expected in white-collar categories (see Figure 2.2). Clerical occupations, which already account for 18 percent of total employment, will provide 16 million jobs for new entrants and reentrants in the work force, if the BLS assumptions hold. Nonhousehold service occupations are likely to account for an additional 10 million openings, nearly as many as in all blue-collar occupations, which together employed more than one-third of the civilian labor force in 1974.

Figure 2.2
Projected Increase or Decrease in Job Openings*
by Major Occupational Group, 1974 to 1985

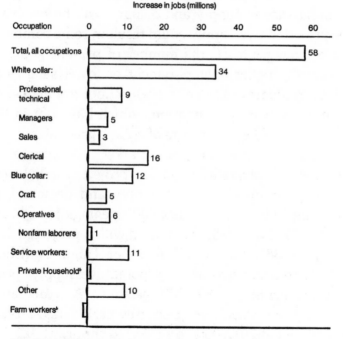

Increase in jobs (millions)

Occupation	Value
Total, all occupations	58
White collar:	34
Professional, technical	9
Managers	5
Sales	3
Clerical	16
Blue collar:	12
Craft	5
Operatives	6
Nonfarm laborers	1
Service workers:	11
Private Household⁴	
Other	10
Farm workers⁴	

*/ Growth plus replacement needs
⁴/ Less than 500,000
Source: Carey (1976), p. 19.

The Market for College Graduates

Of 57.6 million additional job openings expected by 1985, the number of college graduates needed is 12.1 million, or 21 percent of the total (Carey, 1976, p. 20). Over half of these (53 percent) will replace incumbents who retire or die. Another 29 percent represent employment growth in occupations typically held by college graduates. Less than one-fifth (19 percent) reflect continuation of the historic trend of educational upgrading in occupations which in the past have not typically required a college degree. On the supply side of the labor market, 13.1 million college graduates are expected to enter the civilian labor force. Thus, prior to adjustments, an oversupply of about 1 million college graduates is calculated.[4] An important question is how the imbalance in supply and demand will be resolved. The projected oversupply could result in some combination of changes in (1) the number of persons going to college, (2) higher unemployment or lower salaries of college graduates relative to high school graduates, or (3) movement into occupations which have not in the past employed large numbers of college graduates.

Recent changes in the market for doctorate manpower illustrate how quickly projected imbalances place in motion changes in supply and demand.[5] In 1975, the BLS projected 187,400 openings for Ph.D.s between 1972 and 1985, compared with a projected new supply of 583,400 (U.S. Bureau of Labor Statistics, 1975). The result was an anticipated oversupply, prior to adjustments, of 396,000 persons. A year later, projected openings over a shorter period (1974-1985) were placed at 201,900 and projected supply at 422,900 (U.S. Bureau of Labor Statistics, 1976, p. 21). Thus, the anticipated imbalance declined by 175,000 or nearly 50 percent in one year. Much of the change reflects lower projections of earned degrees at the doctoral level. Aside from Allan Cartter's early forecasts (1965), few observers have recognized the change in supply-demand conditions in this market, which emerged with force in the late 1960s and early 1970s.

At the baccalaureate level, job opportunities for new college graduates over the next 10 years are expected to be substantial in several occupational areas: accounting, engineering, nursing, social work, management, technical sales work, and teaching. Despite no projected growth in teaching between 1974 and 1985, attrition from this large occupational category is expected to cause more openings for teachers than for any of the other occupational groups just mentioned.[6]

The Bureau of Labor Statistics (1976) recently published data on the likely number of openings stemming from growth and replacement needs for 241 detailed occupations which collectively account for nearly 70 percent of total employment and include nearly all occupations that require college or other occupational training. Between 1974 and 1985, seven of these 241 occupations are expected to account for nearly one-fourth of all 58 million openings: (1) bookkeeping; (2) secretaries and stenographers; (3) typists; (4) retail trade salesworkers; (5) building custodians; (6) waiters and waitresses; and (7) nursing aides, orderlies, and attendants. Each is expected to generate over 100,000 openings per year. The largest occupation, secretaries and stenographers, may have openings of over 400,000 per year.

In terms of relative growth, only the last occupational group, nursing aides and other hospital attendants, is expected to employ an additional 50 percent or more people in 1985 than in 1974. (In each of the other occupations the bulk of projected job openings will stem from the need to replace workers who leave the labor force.) Twenty-nine of the total 241 occupations will employ at least 50 percent more people in 1985 than in 1974, including three in the health services: nursing aides, orderlies, and attendants (123,000 annual openings); registered nurses (71,000); and licensed practical nurses (93,000). Including RNs and LPNs, but excluding nursing aides, the remaining 28 rapid-growth occupations are expected to account for only 6.4 percent of total openings to 1985. These 28 vary by the level of education typically required of new workers. At one extreme are jobs often calling for four years of college, such as systems analysts, petroleum engineers, and rehabilitation counselors. At the other end are a few occupations which call for little specialized preparation off the job and generally involve government policies, such as wastewater treatment plant operators and asbestos and insulation workers. In between are several occupations for which one or two years of specialized schooling are often desirable: ophthalmic laboratory technicians, state police officers, operating engineers, surveyors, computer service technicians, industrial machinery repairers, medical record technicians and clerks, optometric assistants, respiratory therapy workers, occupational and physical therapist assistants and aides, dispensing opticians, and social service aides. Most of these occupations — in addition to most of the seven largest occupations noted earlier — require some form of upper secondary or lower postsecondary training. Some, however, are commonly learned on the job.

Supply and Demand: The Adjustment Process

In the labor market for college-trained manpower as well as the market for persons with very little education or training, demographic and other developments have spurred considerable discussion of what lies ahead. Freeman (1976), among others, sees a continuing problem of the economy absorbing college graduates, at least in occupational traditionally held by them. In contrast, Wool (1976) and others see a possible shortage of persons willing and able at existing wage rates to perform tasks requiring little formal preparation: hospital attendants, construction laborers, and household workers. Since 1960, youth and adult women reentrants to the work force have filled many of these positions, somewhat replacing blacks and immigrants.

Freeman (1976, p. 11) points out that real starting salaries of people with a B.A. degree have declined since 1968 or so. He notes than when interviewed in October 1972, 45 percent of new college graduates had earnings below their expectations, whereas only 11 percent were earning more than expected (p. 13). Freeman rules out the recession of the 1970s as the explanation for the recent college market bust, agreeing with Gordon (1973) and others on the importance of the intersection of two other trends: (1) rapidly increasing expenditures in several college-trained industries (teaching, research and development, and aerospace) weakened in the late 1960s but (2) the number of college graduates seeking work swelled. Between 1969 and 1976, the number of college graduates in the civilian labor force increased by one-third, from 12.6 to 16.5 million. The number of high school graduates rose by a scant 1.4 million, from 38.4 to 39.8 million.

31

Several potential adjustments — both long and short term — may resolve the imbalance in supply and demand. Relative wages may decline in occupations traditionally filled by college graduates. Unemployment among the college educated may increase relative to others. New graduates may displace those with less education in jobs not typically filled by degree holders — thus putting pressure on high school graduates along the lines suggested by Thurow's (1969, 1974, 1975) job competiton model.[7] Unless job restructuring occurs, such occupational assignment may mean lower remuneration for college graduates and dissatisfaction because of unrealized occupational aspirations. This issue is discussed in Section 4 of this report.

Changes in job opportunities, relative wages, and the availability of different kinds and levels of womanpower and manpower will lead in time to changes in the behavior of employers (e.g., hiring decisions) and of potential workers. Conventional economic theory suggests that if the rate of pay that new college graduates can earn falls relative to that of high school graduates, some youngsters will choose not to go on to college. To illustrate, the market for college graduates may have been in approximate equilibrium in the period prior to the recent downturn (see Figure 2.3). Let us assume the market cleared at a starting rate of pay of W_{68} per year relative to the average wage of high school graduates. That is, all graduates seeking college-level jobs obtained them, and employers had no remaining vacancies to fill with nongraduates. Since 1968, two things have happened. With more college graduates in the labor market, supply shifted from S_{68} to S_{76} by 1976. Demand did not keep pace, moving from D_{68} to D_{76}. The implication of this change is that earnings, adjusted

32

for price level changes, declined — even relative to the earnings of high school graduates (not shown) — and the excess supply of people $(Q^1_{76}-Q_{76})$ was unemployed, stayed home, went on to graduate school, or moved into other markets to compete with those with less education.

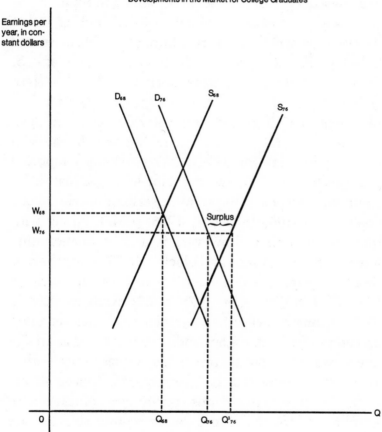

Figure 2.3
Developments in the Market for College Graduates

Earnings per year, in constant dollars

D_{68} D_{76} S_{68} S_{76}

W_{68}

W_{76}

Surplus

0 Q_{68} Q_{76} Q^1_{76} Q

Person years of service

33

This illustration, of course, greatly oversimplifies reality. Most people make decisions based on a longer perspective than one year's earnings. Anticipated lifetime earnings, properly discounted, would be better than a single year's salary. People also have nonpecuniary expectations: job security, the nature of the work, lifestyle, and the like. Nevertheless, the illustration serves to highlight adjustments which one might expect as a consequence of changes in demand and supply.

To add contextual detail, it is worth noting recent developments in campus recruitment by business and industry. For approximately 30 years, Dr. Frank S. Endicott, Placement Director Emeritus at Northwestern University, has issued an annual report, "Trends in Employment of College and University Graduates in Business and Industry" (The Endicott Report). In the 30th Endicott Report (for 1976), 225 companies reported plans to hire 13,500 new bachelor-level graduates. By contrast, the same number were seeking nearly 25,000 graduates in 1968 (Shaeffer, 1976, p. 47). Along with the overall decline, however, is a shift in recruiting interest toward women and blacks.[8] In 1975, for the first time, expected starting salaries for women exceeded those of men (Schaeffer, 1975, p. 69), while as recently as 1964, one of every four women graduates recruited on campus by business and industry was hired as an airline stewardess, market researcher, or secretary — that is, in occupations that do not require a college education. The change in campus recruitment coincides with enrollment trends. More women and blacks are attending college, while the rate of college attendance among white males has declined since the late 1960s.

State of the Art in Manpower Forecasting

Projections of the future demand for and supply of labor have several possible uses. (1) They assist policy makers with decisions in educational policy and in health, energy, and related areas where the availability of human resources is important in determining the ultimate impact of expansion or contraction of programs. For example, the supply of health-related personnel will affect the price of health services and the range of individuals to be served under proposed national health insurance plans. (2) Manpower projections allow adjustments in the educational offerings oᶠ schools and colleges and in admissions criteria. (3) Large employers find projections of value in determining their recruitment, selection, and training strategy. (4) Prognostications may be important to individuals contemplating their career and educational options.

Projections of the Bureau of Labor Statistics, while often lacking the detail required at a local level, are comprehensive and take into account trends in labor productivity; the number of persons in the labor force; the way in which households, businesses, and governments are likely to spend their money; the implications of expenditure patterns of one industry on another (for example, steel needed to produce automobiles), and the probable way in which firms will organize to produce goods and services. Because BLS projections are global in nature, at a highly aggregative level they are reasonably accurate. However, in terms of specific occupations they are often wide of the mark. It is one thing to project the direction and general magnitude of change in major occupational groups such as "professional and technical occupations" and "nonhousehold services"; it is quite another to anticipate growth in a specific occupation, such as elementary school teaching, aerospace engineering, barbering, or police work. Accuracy for any specific occupation requires a special study.

Swerdloff (1969) reviewed the BLS projections for the 1960s, and reached the following conclusions: The Vietnam War, which had not been predicted, had a significant impact. The number of women in the work force increased faster than expected. Industry projections were off somewhat. Growth in construction activity — and thus in construction jobs — increased less than expected. Employment projections in broad occupation categories were reasonably accurate, while those for some specific occupations were off: government and service employment increased more than anticipated; household worker jobs declined more than projected.

Personick and Sylvester (1976) recently reviewed BLS projections for the 1970s and arrived at a comparable conclusion: the projections are accurate at a high level of aggregation. Once again, construction employment grew less than expected; employment in communication and trade was up more than anticipated; and the number of women in the labor force continued to grow faster than predicted.

Projections of manpower supply and demand have been criticized on several grounds. In a recent review of the state of the art in manpower forecasting, Kelley and his associates (1975, p. 46) concluded that "Complex predictions are little more than best guesses," because of difficulty in forecasting collective choices (such as major governmental decisions), the apparently random character of technical change, and the absence of manpower criteria in the formulation of public policy.

Others are critical of the nonuse or misuse of forecasts, and attribute part of the problem to inconsistencies between forecasts and experience. In a recent study of the extent to which vocational educators use manpower data for program decisions, Drewes and Katz (1975, p. 115) found that "The prevailing philosophy seems to be that as long as students continue to enroll in a program, the program will be offered." On the basis of interviews in ten states, the authors found that student interests, faculty suggestions, advisory committees, and employer or professional associations generally prompt consideration of new programs. If manpower data support these new programs, the data are used. If not, local surveys and other data are brought to bear.[9] Once initiated, few if any programs are terminated. Low cost, high likelihood of placement, and student interest appeared to determine program continuation. Drewes and Katz observe: "Several local directors told us of programs in their schools which had high placement rates while manpower projections showed little or no need for additional trained personnel coming from such a program." The fact is, there are several valid reasons for limited use of national manpower forecasts in local program decisions. As Young (1973) indicates, simply knowing whether the number of jobs in an occupation is likely to expand is not all that useful to educators. Many occupations for which preemployment training is appropriate — for developing entry-level skills — have high turnover characteristics, which may not be a consequence of abnormally low rates of pay. Many clerical, health-related, and service occupations (for example cosmetology) are illustrative. Additionally, many students enroll in vocational courses to further interests in hobbies, to acquire do-it-yourself skills, enjoy companionship of friends, or other nonvocational reasons. Automobile and airplane mechanics are examples. Finally, there is the argument that if skills have some general usefulness and are not excessively costly to develop, it makes sense to attend to expressions of student interest.

One shortcoming of the BLS projection methodology is that it makes no allowance for occupational mobility, either as a cause of job openings or as a source of manpower to fill vacancies as they occur. Data from the 1970 census provide the first comprehensive measurement of the extent and pattern of transfer from one occupation to another (Sommers and Eck, 1977). Comparison of work status and occupation in 1965 with similar data for 1970 indicates that movement from one occupation to another is actually a more important source of job openings than attrition. One-third of those working in 1965 moved to a different occupation by 1970 — twice the number of workers who left the labor force. From the perspective of receiving occupations, a third of those employed in 1970 had been in a different occupation in 1965. Occupational changers exceeded new entrants and reentrants by a substantial margin. Only 24 percent of the employed in 1970 were not working in 1965.

Of course, the extent of occupational mobility is by no means uniform. In most high-level professional occupations, especially among men, mobility is low. For example, only 5 percent of medical professionals, such as physicians and dentists, moved to a different occupation; over 80 percent remained in the same occupation; the remainder died or left the labor force. At the other extreme, over half the stock handlers and gas station/garage workers of 1965 transferred to a different occupation. Substantial movement out of these traditional youth jobs is hardly surprising. More surprising is the considerable movement among the well educated. For instance, only 36 percent of male elementary school teachers of 1965 stayed in that occupation; 55 percent shifted to another occupation. While published tables do not show where they went, many of the movers probably ended up in counseling or school administration.

Among the strongest criticisms of existing manpower projections are those of Freeman and Breneman (1974) in their analysis of the Ph.D. labor market. They identify four major sins of omission in past forecasting efforts: "first and most importantly, a failure to consider individual responses to market conditions; second, absence of wage-price phenomena from the computations; third, inability to evaluate the consequences of major policy variables; fourth, failure to take account of the interrelations and feedback processes which govern the market" (p. v). They note that BLS and most other projections are based on continuation of past trends in both demand and supply. In these fixed-coefficient models, projected imbalances in demand and supply do not lead to changes in relative salaries, to changes in school attendance and graduation, or to changes in employer hiring practices. To be sure, the forecasts are accompanied by possible alternative outcomes, but changes in forecasts simply reflect updated trend data as time passes. The net result is that turning points in school attendance from various levels of the educational system and graduation rates from various program areas or majors are rarely predicted in advance.

Freeman's early work on career choice (1971) clearly demonstrates that many markets for high-level manpower — such as law, engineering, and physics — are subject to "cobweb" supply responses[10] to changes in demand. The reason for a four- to five-year cycle is that preparation for these occupations takes several years, and high or low salaries do not set in motion much occupational mobility among those already employed. The data Freeman has analyzed suggest that when job opportunities are abundant and salaries relatively high, an increased percentage of young people will begin preparation for an occupation. When the increased number enters the labor market, the relative salary declines and job openings are less abundant. This dissuades some students from embarking on such a career. As Freeman and Breneman (pp. 43-45) point out, this cyclical disequilibrium results in considerable costs to society in the form of welfare losses.

The Market for Teachers: An Illustration of Forecasting Problems

Earlier in this section, we noted the slowness with which statistical agencies of the federal government have taken into account supply changes affecting the market for Ph.D. manpower. Equally interesting are the dramatic changes which have taken place in the market for elementary and secondary teachers. Throughout the 1950s and 1960s, the demand for school teachers was immense because of burgeoning school enrollments occasioned by the postwar "baby boom." This demographic development had not been anticipated by Seymour Harris (1949), whose dire predictions of an oversupply of college graduates in the 1950s turned out to be wrong.

The availability of teaching positions for those who seek them depends on several factors. Beyond the

number of teaching positions, attrition from the classroom is important. The number of teaching positions
closely follows enrollment levels. Over time, the pupil/
teacher ratio has fallen in a rather steady, predictable
way.[11] Because the enrollment rate for children ages 6 to
16 is close to 100 percent, the number of births largely
determines further enrollments. For a five- or ten-year
period, modest (unexpected) changes in the birth rate
will have relatively little impact, and then only in the
early grades. Concerning attrition from the classroom
(retirements, leaves of absence, promotions to administrative positions), the other significant demand
variable, studies in the 1950s and 1960s placed annual
attrition from the classroom at about 8 percent.

On the supply side of the market, two major sources
are evident : (1) beginning teachers meeting certification
standards who seek to enter teaching for the first time
and (2) reentrants to the work force. Most beginning
teachers are recent graduates. Most reentrants are teachers who have taken a year or more off to bear and raise
children or to return to college on a full-time basis. In
the past, when the supply of certified teachers has been
insufficient to meet staffing needs, employers have
relied on two adjustments to keep the teacher/pupil
ratio from falling as much as it might : they have hired
(1) teachers without degrees or (2) teachers with degrees
but ineligible for standard credentials.

From 1960 to 1972, the number of graduates completing preparation to enter teaching below the college
level (including library science) ranged between 33.5
and 36.3 percent of the total number of graduates
receiving baccalaureates and first professional degrees
(NEA, 1976, p. 2). Each year, about 75 percent of those
eligible to teach went into teaching. It now appears that

41

peak openings for beginning and reentering teachers occurred in 1969. Approximately 179,000 persons entered or reentered teaching that year (NEA, 1972). Peak production of college graduates meeting certification standards, however, did not occur until 1972, when 317,000 were prepared to begin teaching careers. The number of such graduates has declined each year since then, and stood most recently at about 233,500 in 1976 (Chronicle of Higher Education, July 11, 1977, p. 7), a full 30 percent lower than the all-time high. The NEA estimated that in 1976, 185,850 of the graduates wanted teaching jobs but only 94,050 positions were available for them. Furthermore, new graduates were competing with an estimated 117,000 former teachers[12] trying to reenter the profession, plus an undetermined number of previous graduates who were unable to get teaching jobs.

One result of the surplus of teachers is that by fall of 1974, less than half of the eligible June 1974 graduates had teaching positions. By contrast, the rate of successful entry was 74 percent in 1962 (NEA, 1976). A long-term adjustment is evident in the number of freshmen who plan to teach. The American Council on Education's survey of college freshmen reveals that in the fall of 1968, 24 percent indicated elementary or secondary school teaching as their probable career choice. By 1973, the percentage had dropped to only 9 percent. This response, however, had a delayed impact on degrees awarded until 1973, and illustrates the four- or five-year lag noted earlier as typical in markets for college-trained manpower.

Other adjustments are noteworthy. Nearly all openings for teachers now result from turnover rather than growth, since the total teaching force is increasing

42

very slowly, if at all. One might suppose that in a buyer's market, teachers would be less likely than in earlier times to leave the classroom. A projected turnover rate of 8 percent, in other words, may be too high. Two studies — one in St. Louis, Missouri, and the other based on a sample survey of districts — suggests that turnover has, indeed, declined modestly since 1969 (NEA, 1974, pp. 41-43). Such a response should have been anticipated, but the NEA did not reduce its estimate of turnover to 6.3 percent until it reported on fall 1975. A change from 8.0 to 6.3 may seem small, but it implies about 40,000 fewer openings each year. Based on a 1974 study, the U.S. National Center for Education Statistics (NCES) now projects teacher openings based on three alternative turnover rates: 8, 6, and 4.8 percent. The effect of these differing assumptions is clear. Over the period 1976 to 1985, for example, cumulative projected openings total 1.7, 1.3, and 1.0 million, respectively (NCES, 1977, p. 45).

What about changes in quality? A recent study by Weaver (1977), based on SAT, GRE, and similar scores suggests that (1) high school seniors and college freshmen with higher scores (especially verbal) are switching away from teaching as an intended career, and (2) the ratio of acceptances to applicants has increased more in teacher-training programs than in other program areas. Given the overall drop in SAT scores since the mid-1960s, the effect is a significant reduction in the measured aptitudes (especially verbal) of those who plan to teach.[13] Since research by Coleman (1966) and by Jencks and his associates (1972) indicates that teacher verbal ability is one of the few school inputs associated with the attainments of pupils, this qualitative turnaround in the teaching manpower market could result in poorer instructional performance in the future than in the past. It should be pointed out, however, that any deterioration in teacher performance is speculative, since school districts can be more selective than in the past. Unfortunately, data on the teaching abilities of new teachers is not available.

Conclusions

The evidence presented in this section points to the following conclusions regarding the changing realities of the labor market, especially for new, young entrants into the work force:

- The civilian labor force is expected to grow somewhat more slowly between 1975 and 1990 than it did from 1960 to 1975. More importantly, persons 25 years of age and older will account for practically all of the growth to 1990. This is in sharp contrast to the recent past, when youths comprised about one-third of the work force growth between 1960 and 1975.
- While youth will not be the source of net growth in the labor force over the next several years, the absolute number of young people seeking jobs for the first time will remain high until the early 1980s and then will decline only somewhat.
- A sharp turnaround in the demand for Ph.D. manpower and school teachers, both of which rose steadily from the mid-1950s to the end of the 1960s, exacerbated the recent collapse of the market for college-trained manpower.
- Manpower forecasts have been relatively accurate at an aggregate level. However, for particular occupations — especially those requiring baccalaureate, graduate, and professional training — the fixed-

44

coefficient forecasting models now in use fail to reflect responses to supply and demand conditions.

In the area of manpower supply and demand forecasting, several matters warrant increased emphasis:

- Development of a better understanding of employer responses to change in supply-demand conditions — especially job restructuring, choice of persons with different levels and types of education, and choice of older, more experienced workers versus those newly prepared in the same line of work.

- Knowledge of the characteristics of adaptable students and of the pecuniary and nonpecuniary factors which influence choice of field of study and decisions to enter an occupation.

- The development of more sophisticated forecasting models and more timely analyses of likely channels of adjustment when supply and demand are out of balance. This is an especially critical need for occupations for which a college degree is generally required.

- The development of models able to forecast the likely manpower effects of major changes in federal government policy.

------

[1]Throughout this study, the term *adult* refers to people 25 years of age or older, and the term *youth* refers to people 16 to 24 years of age.

[2]The BLS has consistently underestimated increases in female labor force participation and may very well do so again. Given the continuing shift in total employment toward white-collar and service occupations, male workers will have to enter traditionally female occupations if the BLS projections are to be realized.

[3]Until very recently, comprehensive information on interoccupational mobility was nonexistent, and current projections still ignore it. Occupational mobility patterns are discussed later in this section.

[4]The term oversupply in this context simply means that the projected number of college graduates likely to seek work exceeds the number sufficient to maintain past trends, including rates of educational upgrading. The latter term simply refers to increased penetration of college graduates

in various occupations.

[5]In this case the rapidity of change is largely attributable to a lag between actual changes in supply-demand behavior and reflection of such changes in updated projections. The market for doctorate manpower weakened noticeably in the late 1960s and early 1970s.

[6]The market for teachers is discussed in some detail later in this section because it illustrates several difficulties with manpower forecasting.

[7]Educational upgrading of occupations has occurred throughout the nation's history — not solely in response to supply conditions. Indeed, it is taking place more rapidly in blue-collar and service occupations than anywhere else in the occupational structure. For example, median educational attainment among professional and technical workers rose from 16+ in 1968 to 16.5 years in 1976. By contrast, median attainment among non-farm laborers rose from 8.0 to 12.0 years. The reason is that recent high school graduates are quickly replacing the millions of older Americans with even less education as the latter retire or die (Lecht, Matland, and Rosen, 1976).

[8]In a recent report of the Conference Board, Shaeffer (1976, p. 46) writes: "Companies in the latest Endicott survey [30th, 1976] report 12 percent of their on-campus college hires last year were blacks and 20 percent were women. This year the companies plan to make those figures 16 percent for blacks and 27 percent for women. In recent years blacks have made up only 6 to 7 percent of all graduating seniors, so it is plain that major companies are making a concerted effort to hire them prior to graduation. Women are also making real progress, for, as recently as 1972, Endicott surveys showed that only 7 percent of the on-campus hires were female."

[9]In one high school, students wanted programs in aircraft mechanics. Local and regional employment service and BLS statistics were examined and showed little or no need. "Finally, written correspondence with airplane manufacturers over 800 miles away resulted in an expressed need for mechanics" (Drewes and Katz, 1975, p. 37).

[10]This term refers to the path traced by shifts in the demand-and-supply curves described earlier. Shortages spur more people to prepare for employment in an occupation. Some four years later, the supply curve shifts to the right (increases), and relative earnings fall below long-run equilibrium, inducing fewer people to choose the same program in school. A few years later, supply is reduced, earnings are above equilibrium, and so forth. The path of connected price-quantity points looks like a cobweb.

[11]In the early grades, the ratio has fallen since the mid-1960s more rapidly than the longer-term trend in response to programs initiated under Lyndon Johnson's Great Society.

[12]In 1960, the Census of Population counted 304,000 former teachers in the experienced civilian labor force; in 1960-61, 18 percent of this reserve teacher pool reentered teaching. By 1975, the pool was estimated to be on the order of 660,000 (including 29,000 unemployed persons). If about 18

percent wanted teaching jobs, possible reentrants would have totaled 117 thousand.

[13]Weaver, in "Educators in Supply and Demand — Effects on Quality" (*School Review*, August 1978), presents further data based on ACT English and mathematics test scores for 1969-1975 (college-bound high school students) and 1970-1975 (college enrolled freshmen). He points out that other fields of study, in which mathematical and verbal scores have declined to a greater degree include nursing, sociology, and biology (English test scores) and the same fields with the addition of selective engineering (mathematics test scores).

3.
Problems of Youth in the Labor Market

There is no single problem that all youths face in the labor market, yet the employment difficulties experienced by many young people command our concern. As young people proceed through the teenage years to early adulthood, they test the job market, their interests, and their capacities. In this section we concentrate on the unemployment and related problems faced by many young people, especially minority and urban youths and those who leave school before or upon high school graduation.

Youth Unemployment

Unemployment rates among youths tend to be much higher than rates for older, more experienced workers. Table 3.1 shows unemployment rates for various segments of the youth population. Black teenagers — especially those living in poverty areas of the cities and not enrolled in school — have unemployment rates over four times the rate for the entire labor force. Black veterans in their early twenties also have high jobless rates, as do other young veterans, although a figure for whites is not shown.

48

Table 3.1
Unemployment Rate Differentials, 1975

	Unemployment rate Both Sexes	Male	Female
All, 16 years +	8.5	7.9	9.3
All, 16-24	16.1	16.6	15.5
All, 16-19	19.9	20.1	19.7
Black Vets, 20-24	—	26.7	—
Black, poverty metro, 16-19	45.5	—	—
Whites, 16-17	—	19.7	19.2
Blacks, 16-17	—	39.4	38.9
Whites, 18-19	—	17.2	16.1
Blacks, 18-19	—	32.9	38.3
All, enrolled in school, 14-17	—	15.9	17.2
All, *not* enrolled in school, 14-17	—	35.4	36.6

Ratios:

All, both sexes, 16-24	16.1	=	1.9
All, both sexes, 16 +	8.5		
Black vets, 20-24	26.7	=	3.1
All, both sexes, 16 +	8.5		
Black, male, 16-17	39.4	=	4.6
All, both sexes, 16 +	8.5		
Black, poverty metro, 16-19	45.5	=	5.4
All, both sexes, 16 +	8.5		
All, female, *not* enrolled, 14-17	36.6	=	4.3
All, both sexes, 16 +	8.5		

Source: U.S. President (1977).

Youth unemployment has several characteristics different from adult unemployment. First, much of the unemployment of young people is associated with temporary job holding and with entry and exit from the labor force. In 1976, for example, two-thirds of unemployed teenagers had never worked or were reentering the labor force; only 23 percent had lost their last job. In comparison, among unemployed men 20 years of age or over, only one-fifth had been outside the labor force prior to their current spell of unemployment; 70 percent had lost their last job. Among women of comparable age, the figures were two-fifths and 44 percent, respectively (U.S. President, 1977, p. 174). Second, while a sizable fraction of young people experience unemployment, the duration of each spell is considerably shorter, on the average, than it is among older workers.[1] In 1976, while 32 percent of all unemployed persons had been seeking work for 15 weeks or more, the same was true for only 18 percent of unemployed teenagers (pp. 173, 178). Third, when unemployment among adult males is driven to a very low level in response to general economic conditions, the labor market is left with a high residue of unemployment among young people. In 1969, for example, when the overall rate of unemployment was 3.5 percent, the rate among persons at least 25 years of age was close to 2 percent, but was 14.5, 10.5, and 5.7 percent among persons in the 16-17, 18-19, and 20-24 year old age groups. In part, this is a consequence of the responsiveness of young people to economic conditions. When the economy expands, many youths enter the job market who otherwise might stay outside the conventional work force, and the youth-adult unemployment differential rises (see Figure 3.1).

50

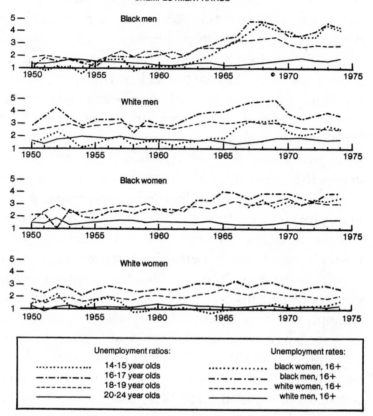

Figure 3.1
Unemployment rates, and ratios of Unemployment rates for
selected segments of the population, 1950 to 1974.

UNEMPLOYMENT RATIOS

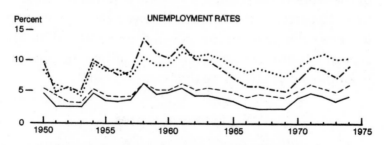

Each ratio refers to the unemployment rate of the age group shown to that
of all individuals of the same sex and race 16 years of age or older.

Source: U.S. Department of Labor (1975).

51

With the possible exception of white teenage girls, the unemployment rates of 14- to 19-year-olds have risen relative to the unemployment rate for all workers in the same sex-race categories 16 years of age and older. Most of the rise occurred from 1963 to 1969, a period of rapid economic expansion. Unemployment of 20- to 24-year-olds has not risen relative to the average for all age groups, except in the case of black men. In other words, the rates for those beyond their teens have moved roughly parallel with the rates for all those in the work force, but unemployment among youths has worsened from two points of view: (1) as joblessness has risen across the board since 1970; and (2) as the number of unemployed youths has increased more rapidly than unemployment in total. While little of this increase reflects a change in the ratio of youth to adult unemployment, the growth of the cohort means more youths are without jobs. In 1955, the average monthly number of persons 16 years of age and over who were unemployed was 2,852,000, or 4.4 percent of the civilian labor force (U.S. President, 1977, p. 148). Unemployed youths 16 to 24 years old accounted for 30 percent of total joblessness.[2] In 1976, the number unemployed stood at 7,288,000 persons, or 7.7 percent of the work force. Jobless youths accounted for close to half (46 percent) of the total. Between these two points in time, the number of persons unemployed in the typical month nearly tripled, while the number of unemployed youths more than quadrupled.

Causes and Cures

What accounts for persistent, high, and — in the case of minority youths — growing unemployment differentials? The causes include lack of marketable skills and work experience; lack of job opportunities for which youths can qualify; relegation of many youths to a "secondary labor market" of unstable, poorly paid, dead-end jobs; discrimination in employment; a weakening of the work ethic; frequent entry and exit from the work force; jobhopping; restrictions imposed by protective labor legislation; and expansion in the relative number of youthful workers.

While there is no one-to-one correlation between causes and potential solutions, it is worth examining some evidence and opinions. Theories of unemployment and suggested solutions are typically interrelated but are only one consideration to emerge in policy formulation. Another issue is whether high unemployment rates among teenagers in school and among others without family responsibilities is a serious problem. Evidence on this point is lacking. Kalachek (1969, p. 5) notes that, "One of the major criteria for evaluating the initial labor market experiences of teenagers should be the impact of these experiences on subsequent adult performance. However, the literature leaves this crucial relationship almost totally unprobed." Freeman (1977), in a recent paper prepared for a conference on youth unemployment sponsored by the Congressional Budget Office, supports this view. A second consideration is the impact of policy on other economic goals such as avoiding acceleration in the rate of inflation. There is little question that an expansion in the economy can add importantly to the employment of youths, but elasticity in the youth labor force, high turnover rates, and other characteristics of youth labor markets would very likely leave youth unemployment rates at a high level.

Research and experience to date leave unanswered many policy questions regarding youth unemployment. Are more public service jobs part of the answer? Will emphasis in school on employability and basic and vocational skills help? Do unemployed youths need counseling and relocation assistance? Are work-education programs part of the answer? Do they need job placement assistance? Are new labor market intermediaries, such as Willard Wirtz's Education Work Councils, needed to help solve the problem? Would a separate minimum wage for youths help? Should certain restrictions on child labor be lifted?

Federal and state statutes and administrative rulings impose constraints on hours, wages, and type of work for those under 18 years old. Except for excluded categories (such as work on family farms, babysitting, caddying, newspaper delivery), work for those under 14 is generally prohibited and is strongly limited at ages 14 and 15. At ages 16 and 17, the laws have some effect. While occasional cases of exploitation arise, the National Committee on Employment of Youth (1975, p. 11-4) concludes: "Work, and by this we mean legal work, has become far safer for young people than inter-scholastic athletics, or the family car," a position supported by Stromsdorfer's (1973) empirical research on the effects of the Department of Labor's experimental Work Experience and Career Exploration Program (WECEP).

A study by the U.S. Bureau of Labor Statistics (1970) suggests that child labor laws may seriously restrict employment opportunities for youngsters under 18. "The most important factor in all cities affecting employers' decisions to hire teenagers under 18 years old was legal restrictions on hiring youth for hazardous jobs." In addition, "legal restrictions" were considered to be the most serious objection of employers to hiring 16 and 17 year olds (p.93). An earlier study by the Stanford Research Institute illustrates that child labor restrictions need not be real, but only perceived, to be an impediment: "On the basis of the fieldwork findings, it is concluded that these many variations and intricacies of child labor laws probably have little effect on the work opportunities of youth except insofar as they serve to confuse labor and school officials and employers" (cited by NCEY, p. 11-5).

One of the most intriguing findings from the NCEY employer interviews is that restrictive child labor regulations may be just an alibi, hiding other, more fundamental reasons for employing teenagers only in "youth jobs" or not at all. "Respondents maintained that legal requirements were an important general reason for not hiring youths, yet a majority (64 percent) claimed that child labor laws were not the impediment to hiring in their own firms" (NCEY, p. 1-2).

A related issue in the youth unemployment puzzle is minimum wage legislation. Since 1938, under the Fair Labor Standards Act, a uniform minimum wage standard has been in effect. Its coverage in terms of types of employment has been extended several times. Many states have lower wage minima for sectors and occupations not covered under the federal law. In principle, of course, if an effective wage minimum exceeds the value of a person's contribution to the production of goods and services, there will be a reduced demand for the particular category of labor in question. The absence in the United States of a special youth minimum has generated a great deal of interest, since youthful workers without substantial work experience or skills might be expected to bear the brunt of whatever unemployment occurs. As Gramlich (1976, p. 410) points out, in 1975, the federal minimum wage of $2.10 per hour was equal to less than half of average hourly earnings in private nonagricultural employment, but was 94 percent of the median wage of employed teenagers.

The effects of minimum wage legislation are by no means clear, yet rigorous analyses point to some negative effect on youth employment and some increase in youth unemployment. Welch (1976) concludes, for example, that increased coverage under the federal minimum wage law has reduced employment of youths, although the effect has been masked to a considerable extent by other forces. Gramlich (1976), using data from the Current Population Survey, shows that minimum wage legislation reduced full-time employment — a matter of considerable interest, given concern that many youths are consigned for an extended period of time to a "secondary labor market" of dead-end, low-paid jobs with little chance for advancment or acquisition of skills. To quote Gramlich (pp. 442-443), "High minimum wages reduce full-time employment of teenagers substantially, forcing many of them into part-time employment. The net result is the relatively slight overall disemployment impact typically found in other studies. If this is why disemployment is so slight, the most reasonable verdict is that teenagers have more to lose than to gain from higher minimum wages. They appear to be forced out of the better jobs, denied full-time work, and paid lower hourly wage rates; and all these developments are probably detrimental to their income prospects in both the short and long run."

Ragan (1977), again using CPS data for the late 1960s and early 1970s, finds that the employment rate of youths has been responsive to increases in the minimum wage and in its coverage. According to his model, "aggregate youth employment would have been 225,000 or 3.3 percent higher had the 1966 amendment to the FLSA not been implemented. Nonwhite employment would have been 13.8 percent higher; white employment 2.4 percent higher" (p. 133). Ragan found the influence of the minimum wage on labor force participation to be slight. Hence, the effect on employment is at the expense of unemployment, and is more serious for blacks than whites. It should be noted, however, that growing youth unemployment from 1968 to 1974 cannot be attributed in substantial measure to minimum wage legislation. The biggest change in the law occurred in 1967, and from 1968 to 1974 the minimum level was eroded in *real* terms as a consequence of increases in the hourly wage rates. In other words, other factors — most especially the recession of 1970-71, the stagflation of recent years (since 1974), and the size of the youth cohort — have had a much more dramatic effect on unemployment among young people.

With respect to changes in the work ethic, the effects of greater affluence and other changes in the youth culture on youth joblessness are not clear. As Kalachek (1969, pp. 2-3) has pointed out: "Labor market folklore is replete with tales of teenagers who are inadequately motivated or who insist on unrealistically high wages. However, the relative prevalence of such attitudes and their quantitative contributions to teenage unemployment has never been explored." Feldstein

(1973, p. 4) feels that "The problem is not that [jobs] are unavailable but that they are often unattractive." Some observers suspect that the extremely high and rising rate of joblessness among black youths, particularly in the city, is partly attributable to high income minima from welfare and other programs and a desire to avoid the menial work which historically has been the lot of large numbers of blacks and other minorities. Faulk (1972) analyzed the Parnes data on young women at the height of the Civil Rights Movement and found that controlling for education and other background variables, young black women who were unemployed did not expect higher wage rates than their white counterparts. Borus has analyzed the experience of young men as well. He reports that within a multivariate framework, race is occasionally statistically significant, but on the whole, reservation wage rates are realistic and seem unlikely to have been a significant factor in the unemployment of black youths in the late 1960s.

Based on an earlier and rather thorough review of the literature on the youth labor market, Kalachek (1969) concluded that the large gap between teenage and adult unemployment is traceable not to negative characteristics of teenagers but to a subtle interaction of characteristics of American youth and the social institutions that shape the transition from school to work. American youths are expected to test the job market, and move about. Compared with many other countries, school and labor market intermediaries (such as the U.S. Employment Service) play a minor role in assisting them. However, schools and colleges are increasingly flexible and accomodating to those who wish to alternate periods of study, work, and a combination of the two, thus promoting youth partial employment and periodic unemployment.

It is widely believed that many youths and adults — especially innercity residents and youths with few job skills — have been consigned to an unstructured, secondary labor market of casual, poorly paid jobs disconnected from advancement opportunities. Doeringer and Piore (1971), Gordon (1972), and Bennett Harrison (1972), among others, have drawn attention to the employment problems posed by segmented labor markets. In their view, the number of "good jobs," with opportunities for promotion and skill acquisition, has not kept pace with expansion in the work force, and large numbers of low-income adults, women, and youths have been consigned to "bad jobs" (Wachter, 1974). Many of those who work in relatively "structureless" employment — a term Kerr (1954) used in his famous article on 'The Balkanization of Labor Markets" — are prevented by barriers of discrimination, lack of representation, and the like from getting "good jobs," which in the aggregate are scarce. It follows from this perception of the job market that manpower training and other human capital investments are unlikely to be very effective, at least in the absence of efforts to create more good jobs by extending minimum wage coverage, encouraging employers to provide training and promotion ladders, and, when necessary, by having the public sector create jobs. Segmented-labor-market theorists often conclude that expansionary macroeconomic policies are likely to result in cost and price pressures in place of expanded job opportunities for those traditionally mired in the secondary labor market. The crux of the argument is that barriers between a primary job market (to which most adult male workers are attached) and a secondary market prevent general expansion in the economy from having its hoped-for effect.

There is little evidence of the bipolarity in wage distributions and mobility patterns expected from conception's of a dual labor market (Cain, 1976). However, empirical tests are difficult because of data limitations. Analysts have been forced to use proxy measures, such as level of full-year earnings, to distinguish between primary and secondary jobs. Andrisani (1973) looked at the experience of young men (1) out of school from 1966 to 1968, (2) who had 12 years or less of education, and (3) whose first job after leaving school and 1968 jobs were as wage and salary workers in nonagricultural industries. In the Foreword to Andrisani's report, Parnes (1973, p. iv) summarizes Andrisani's findings as follows: "Although 'impenetrable boundaries' between secondary and primary sectors is a gross exaggeration, it is equally at odds with the facts to believe that equal levels of human capital, motivation, and [labor] demand create equal employment opportunities for blacks and whites or for youths of different socioeconomic status."

Conclusions

The literature on youth employment problems suggests the following conclusions:

- Increased number of youths in the labor force and continuing high youth-adult unemployment differentials have stimulated public concern for unemployment among young people.
- It would seem that high youth-adult unemployment differentials are not a necessary concomitant of

industrialization and of relatively free labor markets, as the experience of other countries shows, but recent events in several European countries raise questions as to whether the past is an adequate guide to the future.

- Youth unemployment falls when business conditions are good and rises in recessions, but even in good times youth unemployment rates are much higher than the rate for more experienced workers. Teenagers, young blacks, young city dwellers, and veterans have rates many times the national average.

- A variety of causes of high youth unemployment have been advanced. The relative contribution of each, however, is poorly understood. This, in turn, may have inhibited the formulation of appropriate public- and private-sector responses to the problem, although there is no necessary relation between causes and cures.

Further research in the following areas would contribute to policy formation:

- Much needs to be learned about the individual and social implications of joblessness among subgroups of youths: teenagers in school, school dropouts, veterans, and young people in inner cities.

- Relatively little is known about the implications of employer hiring preferences and practices for youth unemployment or about the consequences of relaxing child labor standards. Experimentation with ways to offset some of the costs of hiring teenagers, especially those out of school, is needed. Rather than a special youth minimum wage, certain costs of disability insurance and old-age pensions (that is, social security) might logically be subsidized.

[1]Because of frequent exit and reentry to the labor force, teenage joblessness may be more serious than these figures imply to the extent that some youths become discouraged and drop out of the labor force and return later to unemployed status. Duration statistics refer only to an unbroken current spell of unemployment.

[2]Measured unemployment tells only part of the story. Nearly 2 percent of all 16- to 19-year-olds who were not in the labor force in 1976 said they wanted a job but thought they could not get one (President of U.S., 1977). Among the employed, large numbers reported working part time for economic reasons, such as slack work, job changing during the survey, material shortages, and inability to find full-time work. This category included 659,000 men and 641,000 women 16 to 24 years of age.

4.
Consequences of Schooling

Several debates concerning the relationship between schooling and subsequent achievements have emerged or resurfaced since the late 1960s. One debate questions whether individuals (and perhaps society) have overinvested in college. As Jencks and his associates (1972) have pointed out, while years of education is positively related to subsequent annual earnings, the variance in earnings is large. While the unexplained variation may be attributable to unmeasured variables such as school quality, Jencks argues that pure luck in the labor market is also an important factor. A second debate has involved the general decline since the mid-1960s in test scores in upper elementary and secondary grades. Some wonder whether schooling is becoming less effective. A third issue involves the relative emphasis in high schools between general studies and vocational education. Marland (1971), among others, has urged reform of grades K through 12 in order to build links between school and later life work. At the secondary level, the question is raised whether vocational studies are preferable to a more diverse, general option for those who do not expect to obtain a bachelor's degree. In this section, we review evidence bearing on these issues.

The Ability-Schooling-Credential Nexus

It is no simple matter to ascertain the effects of schooling apart from (1) underlying individual differences in ability and (2) the screening function of credentials. Some argue that highest year of school completed simply mirrors ability differences that show up early in a child's life. Credentialism has recently been a subject of considerable debate in both the professional literature and the popular press. Some argue that credentials are used to allocate persons to various jobs wherein the actual educational requirements for adequate performance are far below the credential held. The result is an inequitable distribution of earnings, out of keeping with real contributions to production, and an overstatement of the social returns from investment in schooling. Berg (1970), in his book *Education and Jobs: The Great Training Robbery*, did much to popularize this concept.

Returns on Investment in College

Numerous studies reveal a strong positive relationship between years of school completed and annual earnings. When differences in earnings are considered in relation to investments in schooling (tuition, books, foregone earnings, etc.), the calculated rate of return has not changed much over the past 40 years. Using census data on 1939 earnings, Becker (1964) found a rate of return of 14.5 percent per year among urban whites with a bachelor's degree. Hansen (1963) calculated an annual return of 10.1 percent, using 1949 census data. Taubman and Wales (1973), using data from World War II veterans which enabled them to control for ability and father's education, found a bachelor's degree to be worth 11 percent per year. Hanoch (1967) and Eckaus (1973), using 1959 census data, calculated returns of 9.6 and 12.0 percent, respectively.

How have the economic returns to college changed since 1968? Freeman (1977) calculates that the private rate of return on a college education slipped from about 12.5 percent in 1968 to 10 percent in 1973, and similarly that the social rate of return may have declined from 13 to 10.5 percent. These declines result from a continuing rise in college costs combined with a decline in the earnings of new college graduates vis-a-vis their peers from high school.

There is considerable evidence of "bumping" in occupational assignments, suggesting that the entire cohort of young people, whatever their level of educational attainment, has been affected by the problem of absorbing such a large cohort into a slow-growth economy. In the late 1960s, the relative earnings of college graduates were extremely favorable in the context of recent history, possibly because of a fairly sharp reduction between 1962 and 1969 in the ratio of college graguates to those with exactly 12 years of schooling in the civilian labor force. In the mid-1970s, however, the relatively lower earnings of college graduates may reflect the sharp increase in the proportion of college graduates in the labor force. The earnings of all college graduates relative to all workers has returned to what it was from 1956 to about 1965. But the oversupply of college graduates has not taken the form of a massive increase in unemployment compared with persons the same age with less education.

Rate-of-return calculations depend heavily on assumptions about the future trajectory of earnings of college graduates who have swelled the work force since the late 1960s (Freeman, 1977). Do repeated cross sections of 25- to 34-year olds describe future earnings? Will the fact that some college graduates have "bumped" high school graduates influence their future earnings? As Freeman (1976, p. 56) notes: "Persons in the large graduating classes of the late 1960s and early 1970s may suffer from a relative excess of supply over their entire lives, creating a significant intergenerational problem." An important question is whether large numbers of recent college graduates will eventually get back on track in terms of career progression.

Many observers (Weisbrod, 1964; Bowen, 1977) feel that earnings differentials, properly discounted, understate the average benefits to the individual as a consequence of added years of schooling. For example, Fuchs, in a recent study entitled *Who Should Live?* (1974), notes the strong correlation between health and educational attainment: better educated persons may have better living habits, make better use of medical care, and more rapidly absorb new knowledge likely to improve health (pp. 46-47). A study conducted under the auspices of the North Carolina State Board of Health (reported in U.S. DHEW, 1973) found that the percentage of households with a nutritionally adequate diet increased with level of education; college-trained homemakers served the most nutritionally balanced meals. A part of this relationship may, of course, be a consequence of income, not education per se. Hettich (1972, pp. 191-196) has estimated the monetary savings from efficiency in consumption and its effect on rates of return to college. His most conservative estimate increased the rate of return by almost 1 percent. Others discount such efficiency effects, in part because education alters lifestyles (Michael, 1975, p. 250; Morris, 1976, p. 107).

The sons and daughters of the college educated perform better than their peers in school (U.S. National Center for Education Statistics, 1976, p. 188-191), most likely because of improvements in parenting that stem from education. Social class is a crude proxy for opportunities provided in various homes for youngsters to learn. Yet in nearly all research, social class is moderately correlated with differences in measured ability and strongly related to educational attainments. Indeed, Cremin (1976, p. 68) concludes that research by Coleman (1966), Jencks (1972), and others, which points to little or no relationship between school expenditures per pupil and achievement, does not reveal that schooling is powerless, but that families are powerful.[1] For example, Johnstone (1976) found that among adolescents age 14 to 18 in Illinois, the quality of interpersonal relationships at home rather than family structure per se bore a strong relationship to delinquent behavior and attachment to a delinquent peer group. (Of course, there is a question of which came first.)

Many studies reveal a strong positive relationship between educational attainment and extent of volunteer work. An ACTION report (1975) estimates that 37 million persons 14 years of age and over (18 percent of the total) performed volunteer work between April 1973 and April 1975, amounting to the equivalent of 3.5 million persons working full time for a year. Of those with four or more years of college, 43 percent

67

volunteered during the year in question; among adults with some college, the figure was 32 percent; for high school graduates, 25 percent.

Theodore Schultz (1975) has reviewed a number of studies that suggest that better educated individuals are more creative and adaptive in responding to change. He cites Michael (1972) and others regarding the adoption and efficient use of birth control pills to control fertility. Several studies (for example, Huffman, 1974) of farmers show that the better educated are more successful than others in adjusting to new economic conditions, resulting in higher profits per farm. The rapid decline in test scores of persons preparing to become teachers, noted in Section 2 of this report, offers interesting support to this notion of adjustment. It may well be that brighter students have paid more attention to changing job market opportunities and therefore have moved in greater numbers into nonteaching fields.

On the whole, studies fail to reveal a strong relationship between educational attainment and expressed satisfaction. One reason, advanced by job satisfaction theorists, is that the expressions of satisfaction often reflect a comparison between one's current position and perceived alternatives. Education widens opportunities. Thus, a well-educated person may be more stisfied than someone with less education, but because perceived opportunities are more numerous, this fact may not show up in response to a single question of liking one's work.

Campbell, Converse, and Rodgers (1976), reporting on 2,000 men and women in their recent study, *The Quality of American Life*, indicate that among less educated persons, only those with high incomes evince high levels of satisfaction. For college-educated persons, self-evaluation of well-being was as high for those with low as for those with high incomes. Bisconti (1976) reports similar findings among recent college graduates. Campbell and his colleagues suggest that college graduates may have greater opportunities for career choice, and that many of those with low incomes may see nonmonetary rewards in their work or derive considerable satisfaction off the job in part because of knowledge and skills acquired through advanced education.

Hyman, Wright, and Reed (1975) recently reanalyzed data from 54 different surveys of adults conducted between 1949 and 1971. While they were unable to control for mental ability, they were able to analyze data by social class origin, ethnicity, rural-urban background, and religion. They found a strong relationship between level of education and knowledge, at least up to age 60. "The better educated have wider and deeper knowledge not only of bookish facts but also of many aspects of the contemporary world" (p.58).

Reporting on a Harris poll of older Americans, Havighurst (1976, p. 16) concluded: "In general, we find that the group with a college education is more active, is more achievement oriented, shows greater life satisfaction and acknowledges fewer personal problems of all kinds when compared with the least educated group." No doubt, part of the difference is attributable to factors other than education per se, including the possibilities opened up earlier in life as a consequence of higher earnings.

Returning to youths and young adults, it appears that persons who have gone to college are glad they did, and many of those who did not wish they had. In a recent

11-year follow-up of high school seniors of 1960, Wilson and Wise (1975) report responses to the question "Most people have 'second thoughts' later on, about some decisions they have made. What would you have done differently in the light of what you now know?" Two percent of those with college experience regretted having gone; 30 percent of those who had not gone to college believed they had made a mistake.

The various kinds and degrees of return on a college education has led to increased concern over the job market for college graduates. Large numbers of young people (especially white males) have decided not to attend, and this adjustment to the oversupply of graduates may well continue for some time into the future. Yet it would be shortsighted to conclude that college is a poor investment for many youths and adults. Demographic trends indicate that by the mid-1980s, economic rates of return on a college education may rise as they did in the early and mid-1960s.

Some observers, especially those who feel that educational credentials serve as a screening device for employers, are not convinced that education per se has the effects alleged. The screening hypothesis takes several forms. Some argue that credentials (degrees, diplomas) are a proxy for underlying, real differences in productivity, adaptability, and ability to learn on the job. Employers recruit on the basis of credentials as indicators of attributes which in the past have been found to be of value. This view leaves open the question of whether such attributes would exist apart from educational experience. To the extent the desired characteristics result from the schooling experience, the economic returns are to the educational investment.

Researchers who have been able to control statistically for underlying abilities report that anywhere from 0 to 40 percent of the apparent return on schooling may be related to individual differences in academic aptitude manifest earlier in life (Psacharopoulos, 1973). In recent work using data on twins, Taubman (1976) reports an even larger antecedent ability effect, but his work is clearly exploratory at this stage and may not be valid because the slightest mismeasurement of schooling could throw off his estimates.

Some researchers (Berg, 1970; Bird, 1975) report finding few differences in productivity or earnings of persons who possess different levels of education. Their studies, however, are of differences in earnings among workers in the same firm or occupation. The difficulty with these analyses is that persons leaving the school system at different levels are distributed across the occupational spectrum in differing proportions. To exaggerate a point, it comes as no surprise that a person with a Ph.D. sweeping floors earns about as much (and is about as proficient) as a floorsweeper with an eighth-grade education. Recent generalizations based on news accounts of college graduates driving taxicabs make the same logical error. Bird (1975) cites several cases of self-made millionaires, suggesting that her readers do not need a college education to be successful. While extreme cases are not without interest, they do not support assertions about the more typical relationship between years of schooling and later attainments. No one would assert that only education makes a difference. Yet, among the variables that would logically be expected to reflect differences in individual productivity, years of schooling continually shows up as one of the most salient.

One test of whether credentials per se are important is to see whether completion of the 12th grade or the senior year of college has considerably better returns than completion of only 11 or 15 years of schooling. Recently Layard and Psacharopoulos (1974) reviewed six studies conducted between 1963 and 1973, using a variety of data sources. Each attempted to ascertain whether the rate of return on a bachelor's degree exceeded or fell short of the return on completion of some college. Two of the studies showed higher returns for dropouts than graduates; three revealed the reverse; one showed essentially no difference. Denison (1964, pp. 219-242), using 1960 census data, failed to find the stairstep pattern differences in educational attainment. Finally, based on the NLS (Parnes) data, Kohen and his associates (1977) found no greater returns on high school or college graduation than on completion of the 11th or 15th grade.

Declining Test Scores

Wiley and Harnischfeger (1977) recently reported to Congress on a study undertaken in late 1975, with the help of the Ford Foundation, to examine possible causes and consequences of national test score declines. Since the mid-1960s, test scores have declined for grades 5 through 12, especially in the higher grades, and declines are most pronounced in verbal tests for college-bound women. The authors examined trends on the Scholastic Aptitude Test (grades 11 and 12), the Iowa Test of Basic Skills (grades 5 through 8), the National Assessment of Educational Progress (science and writing, ages 13 and 17), and several other tests of national importance. Results were mixed. Several tests reveal increased scores in the early grades, possibly because of parent involvement in Head Start and other compensatory programs. In the upper grades, considerable variation exists within the verbal area. Basic reading skills are increasing, but the more advanced skills of comprehension and interpretation of complex textual material are on the wane.

Not all the evidence is in, but Wiley and Harnischfeger do say that "changes in the tests and the ways they are scored, and changes in the composition of the groups taking the tests, cannot account more than slightly for the declines that have been observed" (p. 8). The authors were forced to leave open the question whether the following factors might account for the decline:

1. television viewing
2. drug use
3. family structure and interaction
4. close child-spacing and sibling influences
5. changes in the amount of time people spend in school and modifications in the curriculum.

They speculate that the fifth element may be implicated in the test score decline. They note that school absences have increased and that students are taking (1) fewer courses in traditional academic subjects, and (2) more courses that convey knowledge and develop sensibilities not measured by the usual standardized tests. They point out that, according to the National Center for Education Statistics, students are taking fewer courses in traditional history, foreign languages, algebra and geometry, chemistry, and physics. In some cases, specialty courses such as ecology have taken their place. Even allowing for replacement by a more diverse set of specialty courses, the evidence suggests that "secondary pupils actually are taking fewer courses" (pp. 15-16).[2] The question Wiley and Harnischfeger raise is whether gains in new or novel areas offset declines in other valued areas, and they urge a national dialogue on the purposes of secondary education.

An Advisory Panel on the Scholastic Aptitude Test Score Decline, chaired by Willard Wirtz, recently reported its findings regarding falling scores on the SAT since 1963. Over the period since 1970, the Wirtz Panel (1977) found that less than one-third of the decline was attributable to a change in the composition of test takers, while the decline during the 1960s, when women, low-income persons, and minority test takers increased, may have accounted for two-thirds to three-fourths of the drop. The Wirtz Panel drew attention to several possible reasons for the score decline: reduced emphasis on writing, lower expectations at home and school, television viewing, turmoil associated with Vietnam and Watergate, modification in the curriculum, and changes in family stucture and interaction.

Research on test scores in the early grades is also of interest. Leinhardt (1977), reporting on 1974-75 data gathered from 60 second-grade classrooms at nine sites, reports on school process variables found to be related positively to reading and mathematics scores. Employing indices of (1) opportunity, (2) motivators,[3] (3) structure and placement, and (4) instructional events, she found opportunity to learn and motivators to be importantly related to achievement, taking account of measured initial abilities.

Leinhardt (1977, pp. 29-30) also reports a moderately

positive correlation between opportunity to learn and initial abilities, suggesting that teachers find it easier to direct the better student toward further development. Fine (1966) points out that in a considerable number of underachieving schools in the United States, the bulk of class time is devoted to administrative and disciplinary activities. He cites one California school where teachers report two-thirds of their time went for these purposes, and only 15 percent was devoted to instruction.

Vocational Education

Within secondary education, an important issue is the desirable blend of courses and related activities, especially for boys and girls who do not intend to go on to a four-year college. Approximately one-fifth of high school seniors are enrolled in vocational programs; another two-fifths are general program students; the remaining two-fifths are in academic or college-preparatory programs. As one might expect, there are important differences in what "vocational" means for the two sexes. Young men are in predominantly blue collar, skilled manual programs. Young women are typically enrolled in clerical or sales programs. In both cases, only half or so of each student's program is devoted to the development of occupational skills.

In order to ascertain the effects of high school vocational curriculum on educational attainment and labor market success, it is important to take into account antecedent differences between curricular groups in socioeconomic origins, scholastic aptitude, aspirations, and interests. In the NLS (Parnes) data and other studies, college preparatory students stand out in terms of socioeconomic background and mental ability.

However, these relationships are not as clear-cut among students in either a vocational or general program of studies.[4]

Are students in a vocational program as likely as their general counterparts to aspire to college? If not, is it fair to judge their success by how many years of school are eventually completed? After all, if an occupational program meets psychological and other needs, it has made an important contribution. Data from the NLS reveal that among ninth, tenth, and eleventh graders, nearly half the boys in a general program want four or more years of college, while this is true of only one-quarter of the vocational students. Among young women, the comparable fractions are one-third and one-sixth. Among those who stayed in school from one year to the next (1966-67 for boys, 1968-69 for girls), young men in a vocational program — who already had the lowest aspirations as a group — further revised their educational goals downward. By comparison, over four-fifths of the college preparatory students in the base year aspired to a baccalaureate or higher degree, and even more aspired to a college education by the second year. Thus, it' appears that success in school breeds further success.

Vocational educators frequently argue that, especially for youngsters not academically inclined, "hands-on" learning is especially congenial and adds to the value derived from education. Olson and Bruner (1974) point out that schools tend to convey knowledge through symbolic rather than experiential processes — an approach which has "led to a deemphasis of and/or restricted conception of the nature and development of *ability*." Many students attracted to vocational courses doubtless find experiential approaches to knowledge

76

preferable to symbolic learning.

The social/psychological (including motivational) implications of curriculum choice have received relatively little attention. In the NLS, young men were asked to name the course or area of study in high school they "enjoyed the most" and "disliked the most." Because English, history, mathematics and other academic subjects dominate the curriculum, more young men mentioned these areas than a vocational course, with sentiment pro and con divided evenly on nearly all academic subjects. However, in the case of vocational courses, approximately 13 times as many youths mentioned such a course favorably as unfavorably. In part, this is doubtless a consequence of self-selection and choice of electives. It is likely, in addition, that many youngsters enjoy learning opportunities which cluster around acquisition of useful skills. Somewhat fewer black than white youngsters place vocational subjects in their "enjoyed the most" category. Courses in the humanities elicit more favorable reactions. It is not clear what accounts for this difference by race.

Among young women enrolled in high school in 1968, three areas of the curriculum drew a favorable response: humanities (including foreign languages), vocational and commercial subjects, and other subjects (except science, mathematics, and social studies). Five times as many students gave vocational and commercial subjects a positive than negative rating.[5] The least popular area was mathematics with a ratio of "disliked the most" to "enjoyed the most" of three to one.

Vocational programs are often viewed as a way of increasing the holding power of the schools, especially for youngsters who are motivated by practical job concerns. An analysis of the NLS data for young men shows that having enrolled in a vocational program and completed at least tenth grade increases the probability of graduating from high school. However, the positive correlation between practical studies and highest year of school completed (through grade 12 only) may be attributable to movement from general toward vocational programs. As might be expected on grounds of both occupational goals and the terminal nature of many vocational programs, a student in a vocational curriculum is less likely to go on to college than the general student. For all who complete at least tenth grade, the net impact of vocational curriculum is a reduction in highest year of school completed. This finding takes account of differences in socioeconomic origin and scholastic aptitude (Grasso and Shea, 1979).

College is not the only option beyond the high school. By 1969, over 50 percent of out-of-school young men 17 to 27 years of age had received some kind of further occupation-related training outside of college (Grasso, 1975). Some 12 percent had received training in the armed forces. One in 12 reports having participated in an apprenticeship program. One in five had attended a business college or technical institute, and almost as many report having been in a company school of some sort.[6] While not statistically significant, fewer black high school graduates (43 percent) than white reported having further training. The difference in apprenticeship was especially great — 3 percent of blacks versus 12 percent of whites.

Several studies (Reubens, 1974a, 1974b; Stromsdorfer, 1972; Warmbrod, 1968) have reviewed the cost-effectiveness in the labor market of an occupational program of studies for those who do not go on to obtain a B.A. degree. Such research generally shows little effect of curriculum on the labor market success of individuals, as traditionally measured. A National Planning Association study, which purports to show that graduates of vocational programs did slightly better than their academic and general counterparts in 1968, failed to control statistically for scholastic aptitude or socioeconomic background. Using five-year follow-up data from Project Talent, Howard Vincent (1969) found little if any difference in average earnings of graduates. However, taking into account socioeconomic status and mental ability, he did find that vocational graduates had an adjusted hourly rate of pay a few cents higher than general and academic graduates with equivalent years of schooling.

Using data on young men in the NLS, Grasso (1975) compared the labor market experience of students from various curricula who completed exactly 12 years of school. Grasso was able to control statistically for scholastic aptitude, socioeconomic origins, region, and whether a person lived in an urban setting (standard metropolitan statistical area). He found no difference between vocational and general graduates in either beginning rates of pay or in growth in wages over time, with one exception: Noncollegiate training beyond the high school (company schools, apprenticeships, and so forth) made a bigger difference for vocational graduates than for others. With respect to occupational status and job satisfaction, there were no significant differences between graduates of vocational and general programs, except that among the former, the small number who took commercial studies had somewhat higher-status jobs and slightly greater job satisfaction. There were no differences in unemployment experience.

Grasso's finding that post-high school training outside of college seems to pay off more for vocational students than others may mean that some high school programs are good pre-vocational preparation. Two studies support this interpretation. Horowitz and Hernstadt (1969) found that tool and die makers who combined vocational school preparation with apprenticeship reached maximum proficiency earlier and were given better ratings than tool and die makers who learned their trades in other ways. Glover and Marshall (1975) reached much the same conclusion in a study of construction craftworkers. More recent work by Grasso and Shea (1979) indicates that among female high school graduates in the NLS, those who participated in a business or office program enjoyed higher wages and higher status jobs than their peers in other curricula.

Having participated in a vocational or commercial program in high school is viewed positively by young men who completed high school but went no further. In the NLS, for example, young men out of school at the time of the 1966 survey were asked: "Considering all the experience you have had in working or looking for jobs since leaving school, do you feel that not having more education has hurt you in any way?" Among white youths, 42 percent of the general graduates said "yes" but only 29 and 25 percent of the vocational and commercial, respectively, answered "yes" — a statistically significant difference. Among black youths, insufficient sample cases limit the comparison to general and vocational graduates. The percentages answering "yes" were 57 and 70 percent, respectively, suggesting that young black men from a general program feel their education has more adequately met their needs. Because of small sample size, however, this difference could have resulted rather easily from sampling variation.

Thus far, we have only considered high school graduates who have not gone on to complete a year or more of college. Grasso and Shea (1979) report that men and women completing 13 to 15 years of school, regardless of high school curriculum, have higher status jobs and higher earnings than those who have completed only 12 years of school. Since young workers with 12 years of education have more labor market experience than youths of the same age with some college, this difference is noteworthy.

Regarding high school dropouts versus graduates, data from the NLS indicate that male high school graduates are only slightly better off economically than those who left school after completing tenth or eleventh grade. The gap in wages for young women at work, on the other hand, is somewhat greater, suggesting that high school graduation is more important for the kinds of jobs available to women. Data from the October 1973 CPS confirm these findings. Among employed 16- to 24-year-olds not enrolled in school, the distribution of the two groups of men by occupation is quite similar, while the difference among the women is considerable (NCES, 1976b, p. 7).

In evaluating the economic implications of skill training for society, including basic skills, the employer's perspective has been given little attention. It is often assumed that if most programs of formal occupational preparation were to vanish overnight, employers might do the job (and perhaps do it better) at no cost to the taxpayer. There are several issues here.

One is the matter of comparative efficiency in skill acquisition. Another is whether employers have an incentive or capacity to develop skills other than those which are related very specifically to their company's needs. As Margaret Gordon (1964, 1965) points out: (1) the willingness of employers to engage in training depends, in part, on tightness of the labor market; (2) serious issues of equality of access to training arise as a consequence of employer selection any time reliance is placed on on-the-job training; and (3) only large firms are inclined to provide very much training, due to incentives, comparative cost-efficiency, or both.

Conclusions

The vast research of the past twenty years supports the following generalizations regarding the consequences of schooling:

- Years of schooling is by far the most salient variable related to the kind of work people do and to their earnings. While additional years of education do not ensure that a person will have a high status occupation and high earnings, they significantly increase the probabilities.
- There is a positive relationship between years of schooling and extent of volunteer activity, good health practices, effective parenting, consumer efficiency, ability to adjust to change, and satisfaction with nonwork dimensions of life. Moreover, such effects seem to endure over time.
- Highest year of school completed is not an exact mirror of innate individual abilities, but the two are related. Highest year of school achieved accounts for 60 percent or more of the gross relationship between schooling and labor market outcomes.

- Completion of the last year of high school or of college does not add significantly to a person's labor market success compared with completion of 11 or 15 years of formal education. In other words, there is little evidence that educational credentials per se have much impact on a person's earnings.
- The rate of return on a college education has declined somewhat since the late 1960s, but remains comparatively high, especially in view of the enormous recent expansion in the number of college youths in the job market. The rate of return could well increase in the 1980s, when demographic developments will be more favorable to graduates.
- Scores on a variety of standardized tests have declined since the late 1960s or early 1970s — at least above the fifth grade. Declines have been especially noticeable in advanced academic areas such as comprehension and interpretation of complex verbal statements. Neither reasons for the decline nor implications for worklife are entirely clear.
- Choice of (or assignment to) a vocational program at the secondary level as opposed to a general program is related to (1) a lowering of educational aspirations; (2) little or no effect on completion of high school but a reduction in highest year of school completed; (3) higher wages for women graduates who have concentrated on business and office skills and for men who have taken additional training outside regular school; and (4) a greater likelihood of feeling that one's education has been adequate, except for blacks.

A number of questions regarding the consequences of education remain unanswered:

- Knowledge is needed on "work establishment" — that is, the movement of young people from youth jobs to

83

more established, secure positions in the occupational structure. No one is sure whether today's massive cohort of youths will be at a competitive disadvantage their whole lives, or whether more time will simply be needed for large numbers of them to get back on track. Longitudinal research on youths is called for, perhaps supplemented by historical analyses of periods such as the 1930s.

- Past studies of schooling effects, especially those based on large-scale surveys, have been deficient in several respects: aggregation bias, inadequate measures of educational activities, inattention to nonschool variables, and so forth. Research is called for to ascertain whether changes in curricula and in the amount of time spent trying to learn are related systematically to educational achievements.
- Research is needed on changes in test scores as related to such phenomena as changing family life and television viewing.
- More needs to be learned about how colleges and universities, and their academic units, are responding to changes in the composition of their student bodies.
- While a great deal is known about how young people fare in the labor market once they have left regular school, more global effects of education (for example, on productivity, profits, and prices) are poorly understood. Furthermore, relatively little research has been conducted on access to nonformal education and training, and on the implications of such training for earnings and career mobility.

---

[1]Much has been written about the lack of relationship between schooling resources (dollars spent per child) and educational or economic outcomes (Coleman and others, 1966; Jencks and others, 1972). A problem with some of these large-scale studies, however, has been the use of proxies for

resources — such as student/teacher ratios — and lack of disaggregate information — such as measuring school resources by district-wide averages rather than school or classroom figures.

[2]Charles Fowler, superintendent of schools in Fairfield, Connecticut, was quoted in the *New York Times* (May 4, 1977) on this subject. Students in his district were spending an average of 900 hours per year in school compared with 1,000 hours just 25 years ago. Legal holidays, in-service training, parent conferences, and other uses of time have increased.

[3]Opportunity consisted of time available to learn material, measured in terms of: teacher absences, student days in school, enrollment, attendance, chance to start work immediately rather than when the teacher tells everyone to start together, minutes spent on the subject, and number of transfers in or out of the class during the year. Motivators were measured in terms of: additional books for reading; use of games and texts for mathematics; quickness in returning work to the students; chances for cognitive exploration; student choice of materials and how to do the work; *not* letting students decide which subject to study, whether to work alone, or when to take a rest; and student scoring of own tests, use of peer tutoring, and use of praise.

[4]Many of the findings from the NLS reported here are described in greater detail in Grasso and Shea (1979).

[5]For the most part, vocational studies for boys involve agriculture and skilled manual (blue-collar work). For girls, however, the vast majority in programs of occupational preparation were enrolled in secretarial, book-keeping, and other clerical (white-collar) areas.

[6]In a more popular vein, Bird (1975) has advised young people to reconsider their options to include travel and jobs, as well as vocational/technical studies, as alternatives to college.

5.
Work-Education Programs

Since World War II, the proportion of young people combining schooling with paid employment has risen dramatically. Between 1947 and 1975, the labor force participation rate[1] of 14- to 17-year-old male students increased from 22 to 29 percent (U.S. President, 1977, p. 198). Among enrolled men 18 and 19 years old, the rise was even greater: from 25 percent in 1947 to 42 percent in 1975 (Ibid., p. 199). The labor force participation rates of female students rose at an even faster pace. Part of this increase may be attributable to the introduction or expansion of formal programs designed to link schooling with jobs. It is also likely that changes in school calendars and in family life and greatly expanded part-time and temporary job opportunities have encouraged students to combine school with work.

Actual work experience has been a component of federally aided vocational education since the original Vocational Education (Smith-Hughes) Act of 1917. Several new public and private initiatives emerged in the 1960s. The Economic Opportunity Act of 1964 launched the Neighborhood Youth Corps (NYC) and the College Work-Study (CW-S) program, designed to encourage further schooling by meeting the pressing needs of youths from low-income families. For several years, the

Department of Labor has sponsored a special summer jobs program for youths. The Vocational Education Amendments of 1968 added High School Work-Study and Cooperative Education programs, targeted especially to disadvantaged youths. Several other programs have emerged since 1960: a Cooperative Education program for institutions of higher education; a Work Experience and Career Exploration Program (WECEP) sponsored by the Department of Labor, involving relaxed labor standards for 14- and 15-year-olds; and University Year for ACTION. In August 1977, with the signing of the Youth Employment and Demonstration Projects Act, additional programs were established. A Young Adult Conservation Corps was established, along the lines of the preexisting Youth Conservation Corps. $115 million each was set aside for Youth Incentive Entitlement Pilot Projects and Youth Community Conservation and Improvement Projects, with the bulk of the remaining $1 billion for a variety of Youth Employment and Training Programs initiated and operated by prime sponsors under the Comprehensive Employment and Training Act. A most interesting new development is the Youth Incentive Entitlement Pilot Projects, which are designed to demonstrate and test various approaches that will guarantee jobs or training for economically disadvantaged teenagers who agree to stay in school or return to school. Beyond these federally supported programs, there are a wide variety of state, local, or private efforts, including programs which involve youngsters in cross-age tutoring and community volunteer work.

Purposes

Those who support work-education programs tend to

see several values in such efforts: income, learning about the world of work, reducing age segregation, enhancing feelings of accomplishment, and motivating youngsters to stay in school. While various programs may be categorized under the heading of work and education, there are major differences in ostensible purposes and in clientele served. To illustrate, the term *cooperative education* generally denotes programs that have learning as their central goal, wherein educational institutions and employers jointly plan and carry out education and training objectives. Financial rewards for students and employers are usually of secondary importance. In contrast, most *work-study* programs emphasize financial aid and enhanced educational opportunity, with learning a by-product.

Consequences

Nearly all work-education programs generate income for participants, and this income undoubtedly contributes to economic and psychological well-being. The College Work-Study program is usually given high ratings precisely because it has made an enormously important contribution to this major goal — providing income so that low-income students can attend college. Another consequence of work-education programs is that students spend their time differently than they otherwise would, but it is not always clear whether the work component of programs takes the place of less productive uses of time or study time — except in the case of summer jobs and vacation work. In the absence of sufficient unsubsidized summer employment opportunities, it makes sense to most citizens to put otherwise idle hands to work. Since school is not in session, the time spent working — and producing and earning money — does not compete with school work, and keeps some youngsters "out of trouble." In fact, the federally sponsored summer youth program is sustained largely because of the belief in Congress and elsewhere that it is good "riot insurance."

Prior to 1974, the Neighborhood Youth Corps (NYC) was a separate categorical program with three components: an in-school program for youngsters of high school age; a summer component; and an out-of-school component.[2] Many of the studies on these programs are seriously flawed methodologically, and results are mixed. A study of programs for out-of-school youths in Indiana in the mid-1960s revealed favorable earnings gains for men, but not women, relative to a comparison group of nonparticipants (Borus, Brennan, and Rosen, 1970). Robin (1969) studied in-school and summer programs in Detroit and Cincinnati. Reviewing his work, Perry and his associates (1975, p. 94) note: "Since enrollees (in Detroit and Cincinnati) spent time working instead of at their studies, participation in NYC actually impaired grades of enrollees who had previously performed adequately in their studies (at least a C average prior to enrollment)."[3] A study by Somers and Stromsdorfer (1970) revealed, among other things, that the in-school and summer programs seemed to have had no positive effect on the probability of high school graduation except for black females. This lack of impact on scholastic achievement and retention was not expected of the in-school program; the prevailing conception in the early 1960s was that many students from poverty families had to contribute to family income and would leave school to do so if part-time job opportunities around the school were not available. It was hoped that work might also have beneficial effects on school achievement.

Stromsdorfer (1973) examined the consequences of a high school cooperative education program in Dayton, Ohio. His study is of special interest because he was able to (1) devise a comparison group and (2) examine both academic achievement and post-school experience in the labor market. In general, he found positive or neutral effects of cooperative education on labor market outcomes. However, in comparison with the control group, students in the cooperative program experienced a steady deterioration in academic achievement from freshman to senior year.

A recent study conducted by the Olympus Research Corporation (Walsh and Totten, 1976) surveyed 84 special projects in 77 communities in 23 states, financed under the disadvantaged provisions of the Vocational Education Act. At the project and school level, the research uncovered the following: (1) two of every three high school students were enrolled in regular as opposed to special classes;[4] (2) nearly half the students were enrolled in work experience programs; (3) 69 percent of the students participated in projects which did not involve skills training either in the classroom or on the job; and (4) work experience students, for the most part, performed tasks in jobs characterized by low skill, low pay, and high turnover (waitress, dishwasher, service station attendant, general office work, baby-sitting, laborer, and the like). Program completion rates were high (83 percent); student ratings were over-whelmingly favorable, as were employer ratings of students. Nevertheless, the report raises an important issue: Are special program funds for the disadvantaged being used to create a new "lower track" for disadvantaged students — just the opposite of what was intended?

In a companion study of handicapped programming under the Vocational Education Act, the Olympus Research Corporation (1974) reported strong administrative support for "mainstreaming"[5] but frequent extenuating circumstances: auditing problems, need for training of local staff, and the like. In 69 percent of 74 local projects examined as case studies, handicapped students were not integrated even partially into regular classes, despite the fact that three-fifths of the projects were being carried out by vocational or comprehensive high schools. Once again, however, employers, parents, and students were overwhelmingly enthusiastic about the vocational program opportunities. Ninety-four employers (20 percent of the projects) who had hired handicapped program completers or provided work-experience slots were interviewed. Handicapped youngsters were judged no better and no worse than regular workers in terms of absences and productivity, but were given better ratings on punctuality, attitudes, and taking directions.

What about the effects of work-education at the post-secondary level? In a study of 65,000 participants in the National Youth Administration (NYA) in 1938-39, working students received higher grades than other students (Federal Security Agency War Manpower Commission, 1944). In a recent, small-scale study of work-study freshmen at the University of Colorado, Adams and Stephens (1970) discovered that CW-S students performed better academically than the freshman class as a whole. They attributed the difference to more effective organization of time. Augsburger (1974) sought to determine the influence of part-time employ-

ment on the academic performance of full-time undergraduate students on academic probation. Two of his
findings are important here: (1) Students — whether on
campus or off — who worked 20 hours or less per week
had significantly higher fall term GPAs than students
who did not work (2.39 versus 2.20). (2) The small
number of probationary students who worked more
than 20 hours per week had significantly lower fall
GPAs than other working or nonworking students.
However, because only 12 students worked off campus
more than half time, Augsburger suggested the need for
further investigation of the hours-per-week finding.
Augsburger also called attention to the fact that a
number of other investigators (Trueblood, 1957;
Henry, 1967; and Budd, 1956) found no adverse effect
of part-time employment on academic performance. At
least one (Henry), however, reached a conservative conclusion regarding freshmen in need of financial aid —
namely, that they need not sacrifice academic achievement if they are employed 15 hours per week or less.
Two other pieces of research cited by Augsburger (Hay,
1969; Baker, 1941) revealed adverse effects on academic
performance for students who worked over 15 or 27
hours per week, respectively.[6] These findings are similar
to those of a review by Oscar Lenning and his associates
at the American College Testing Program (1974). Based
on data published in the 1960s, they concluded (p. 12):
"Extracurricular activities (including work) do not seem
to inhibit and may assist academic success if the activity
is not concentrated to any great extent. Overconcen-
tration on an out-of-class activity, however, can interfere with academic progress."

MacGregor (1966), in his study of Brooklyn College
undergraduates, found that half of those who did not

work made the choice because they feared employment would interfere with their academic work or co-curricular activities and that one in four working students felt that employment lowered their grade point average or otherwise interfered with their learning.

Does work (and learning at work) ever contribute positively to academic achievement? The argument is rather compelling that cooperative education programs, especially ones which alternate periods of full-time work and study and have specific occupational performance objectives, may yield significant benefits. Even in career exploratory programs, students generally report such immediate benefits as a chance to explore options and to test a tentative career choice or field of specialization.

The most complete evaluation of the College Work-Study Program to date was carried out by Columbia University's Bureau of Applied Social Research in 1970-71 (Friedman and others, 1973). One in four of the approximately 8,000 students who responded to their questionnaire survey cited as a job disadvantage "little time for studying," and 35 percent felt their "grades would be better if [they] didn't have to work." Nearly a third noted little time for athletics or extracurricular activities. One in five said the same for family or friends. Friedman and his associates did not, however, examine grade point averages.

Nearly two-thirds of the approximately 8,000 CW-S students who completed questionnaires were involved in clerical, library, security, maintenance, food service, and hospitality aide work. In most cases, young men and women were assigned to jobs traditionally performed by members of their sex. Only 15 percent of the students surveyed worked as teaching or research assistants, social or community aides, or government and judicial aides — jobs given high ratings by students. Work assignments were perceived to be "major-related" or "career-related" by only 27 and 23 percent of students, respectively.[7]

Over half the CW-S students surveyed said they were "very satisfied" with their jobs. Very few expressed dissatisfaction. Nearly all students agreed that they "made friends and learned about people." Over half said their jobs required intelligence and judgment. Two-thirds noted a responsibility dimension in their work. Nearly half cited "doing something worthwhile" as an advantage of their job. Two out of three indicated that they "acquired skills useful for a career." Only one in four, however, expressed greater "certainty about a career choice"; and 6 and 8 percent, respectively, cited as job disadvantages "confusion about career" and "disillusionment about work."

Some jobs, of course, tend to be rated higher than others. CW-S assignments seen as "major related" or "career related" were more often cited favorably in terms of acquisition of useful skills, doing something worthwhile, and clarifying career choice. Concerning the latter advantage, half of the students in career-related jobs felt the experience had made them more certain about their career choice, compared with only 20 percent in jobs not viewed as career related.

Certain characteristics tend to distinguish highly rated jobs from others. In addition to being major or career related, they are frequently (1) found by students on their own or chosen by students from an array of possible assignments, (2) off campus rather than on campus, and (3) flexible in terms of offering the possibility of a student arranging his or her hours.[8] In addition to teaching or research assistants, social or community aides, or government and judicial aide positions, positions in athletics, tutoring, and newspaper work are also rated highly.

Over 2,000 employers or supervisors of CW-S students were queried, and their perceptions of benefits were highest among those who needed CW-S workers and who provided "jobs with a high level of skill and with relevance to the academic and career interest of students" (Friedman and others, 1973, pp. 6-7). While nearly all employers viewed the CW-S program favorably, the proportion reporting that students developed useful skills was substantially higher among those "who provide jobs which take the longest time to learn, who supply job descriptions, or who are able to place students in interest-related work" (p. 242).

High student ratings correlate to some extent with the perceptions of college administrators. Students surveyed by Friedman and his associates tended to rate their jobs more highly on campuses where administrators saw their highest goal as "making college more relevant" or "expansion of college services."

With regard to work-education and performance after graduation, Cross (1973, p. 18) mentions three studies at the college level which compared the performance of co-op with non-co-op students. The first, by Gore (1972), found no difference in starting salaries of the two groups from the University of Cincinnati's College of Business Administration, but an advantage to the former in terms of growth in earnings and job status over time. A study by Wilson and Lyons (1961) revealed higher GRE Advanced Engineering test scores for co-op students. Yencso (1971) reported higher grades of co-op alumni compared with their non-co-op counterparts.

In well-designed cooperative programs, one would expect employers to benefit as well as students.[9] In 1974, a research team from Arthur D. Little, Inc. sought "to document and, where possible, quantify the benefits employers realize from cooperative education" (1974, p. i). Officials were interviewed in six organizations committed to cooperative education and known to manage their programs effectively. (The six employers were General Electric, Xerox, the Social Security Administration, a public school system, a bank, and an insurance company.) In the first "preprofessional" employment phase of the program, employers derived benefits such as redesigning jobs of professionals by providing them with assistants or reorganizing positions so as to reduce the amount of time professionals spend on time-consuming, routine tasks. The resultant increase in productivity apparently exceeded expenditures on the co-op students. While such students typically were paid entry-level wages, (1) growth in the beginning salaries of co-op workers was moderated; (2) time-in-grade increments were avoided; and (3) employers saved on fringe benefits. Some employers felt that "their programs could be economically justified solely from financial benefits of this type." More cost-effective recruitment and a better match between employer and professional employee were other benefits often cited. Employers could look over and evaluate potential permanent employees. More than one employer stressed the importance of cooperative education in obtaining access to minority talent.[10] Other benefits included better retention; reduced cost of training and orientation for work-study students who became permanent employees; greater immediate value to the employer; and feedback to college faculty and counselors. The latter was said to improve college performance and to benefit the employer and students as well.

ACTION, the nation's program of voluntary service, initiated a service-learning program in cooperation with universities — University Year for ACTION — in which students from participating institutions work full time for a year in a variety of anti-poverty projects. In addition to small stipends, some of which are financed through CW-S, students receive regular academic credit from their college or university. Projects include (1) community economic development efforts, such as the resuscitation of a credit union (University of Missouri, St. Louis — Union Sarah Community Corporation); (2) tutoring and other assistance for immigrant youths (University of Hawaii); (3) efforts to improve the health of adolescents (City University of New York); and (4) many other local projects around the country. In terms of what students derive from their efforts, John Ganley, Deputy Director of ACTION, says: "In a survey taken of volunteers who had completed one year of service, 97 percent said they learned more from a year in UYA than from a comparable year of traditional education. In a survey taken of seven UYA schools, it was found that 75 percent of the job assignments were career related" (see Committee on Education and Labor, 1974, p. 123).

Griliches (1977) recently reported on an on-going investigation of the consequences of interruptions in schooling ("stopping out") and of work while in school, using data on young men from the Parnes survey. Much of the interruption studied was associated with military service. Several findings are of interest. First, of those who worked while in high school, only 7 percent reported that it interfered with their schooling, and for them there is no evidence that this adversely affected subsequent earnings. Second, more advantaged youngsters were "likely to work more frequently but slightly less intensively than less advantaged youth" (p. 14), a finding corroborated by unpublished tabulations from the National Longitudinal Survey of the Senior Class of 1972. Third, accumulated work experience during high school had no significant effect on subsequent wage rate, while work in college had a mild positive influence. Fourth, based on the NLS of 1972, little relationship was found between extent of school homework and paid employment among seniors in high school, leading Griliches to conclude: "Engaged in moderation, they do not seem to impinge on each other." Finally, the analysis revealed no effect of school interruption on subsequent earnings. Thus, there is no evidence that stopping out of school involves additional costs to the individual beyond the direct cost of having postponed additional educational attainment. Results of the various studies presented in this section are summarized in Table 5.1.

Table 5.1

Summary of evaluation studies of work-education programs

Study	Subjects	Findings	Whether Confirmed
		SECONDARY STUDENTS	
1. Borus, Brennan, and Rosen (1970)	NYC, out-of-school partici-pants, Indiana	Positive earning gains for males, but not females; greater effect for dropouts than graduates	
2. Robin (1969)	NYC in-school and summer participants; Detroit and Cincinnati	Negative effect on school grades	Yes (See #6)
3. Somers and Stroms-dorfer (1970)	NYC in-school and summer participants; national sample	No positive effect on retention in school, except perhaps black females	
4. Walsh and Totten (1976)	Vocational education projects for the disadvantaged	Generally positive attitudes but little skill training	Yes (See #5)
5. Olympus Research Corp. (1975)	Vocational education projects for the handicapped	Generally positive attitudes, but little integration with nonhandicapped peers	Yes (See #4)
6. Stromsdorfer (1973a)	High School cooperative pro-gram, Dayton, Ohio	Positive or neutral economic impact; negative on grades	Yes (See #2)

COLLEGE STUDENTS

Study	Sample	Finding	
7. Federal Security Agency War Manpower Commission (1944)	College students in National Youth Administration, national survey	Positive effect on grades	Yes (See #8)
8. Adams & Stephens (1970)	CW-S freshmen, U of Colorado	CW-S positively related to grades	Yes (See #7)
9. Augsburger (1974)	Undergraduate students on academic probation, Northern Illinois U	Students who worked 20 hours or less per week had higher grades in subsequent term; those who worked 21+ hours had lower grades	Yes (See #15 & #16)
10. MacGregor (1961)	Brooklyn College undergraduates	Choice of not working related to likely impact on grades; one-fourth of working students thought work interferred with their studies	
11. Friedman and others (1973)	CW-S students, national sample	Generally positive perceptions of personal and economic impacts (see text)	
12. Trueblood (1957)	Indiana University students	Working students had higher GPA but not statistically significant	Yes (See #13 & #14)
13. Henry (1967)	University of Missouri freshmen	No difference between working and nonworking students in GPA	Yes (See #12 & #14)
14. Budd (1956)	Freshmen at Western Washington College of Education, with low mid-term grades	No significant difference between working and nonworking students	Yes (See #12 & #13)

Study	Population	Findings	Effect
15. Hay (1969)	Information not available	Work over 15 hours per week had adverse effect on academic performance	Yes (See #9 & #16)
16. Baker (1941)	Friends University undergraduates	Work over 27 hours per week had adverse effect on academic performance	Yes (See #9 & #15)
17. Gore (1972)	Co-op graduates, U of Cincinnati College of Business Administration	No difference in beginning salaries, but co-op advantage in growth in salaries and job position over time	
18. Wilson and Lyons (1961)	Co-op students in engineering, business administration, and liberal arts; several institutions	Higher GRE scores in engineering; co-op students saw work as clarifying goals	Yes (See #19)
19. Yencso (1971)	Co-op alumni in engineering from four colleges	No difference in economic outcomes; co-op alumni had higher GPA	Yes (See #18)
20. Arthur D. Little (1974)	6 co-op employers	Significant benefits reported by employers	
21. ACTION UYA study (1974)	Participants in University Year for ACTION	97 percent of participants perceived learning more than they would have in college	

SECONDARY AND COLLEGE STUDENTS

22. Griliches (1976)

Respondents in NLS (Parnes data) and in NLS of Senior Class of 1972

No significant impact of work or school interruption on subsequent earnings; mild positive effect of work while in college

Conclusions

Studies of work-education programs suggest the following conclusions:

- Work-study programs can have a detrimental effect on academic achievement if (1) a student has difficulty meeting the demands of the educational program alone; (2) the work is essentially unrelated to the school program; and/or (3) hours of work exceed about 20 hours per week. However, work that is related closely to the academic program can have beneficial effects on academic achievement. Student motivation and habits of self-discipline may also affect this relationship.

- Most work-education programs add to earned income and to nonacademic achievements. Students, parents, and participating employers generally view work opportunities linked with schooling positively.

- The long-term consequences of combining work with education are less certain. There is no evidence that such programs reduce earnings, and for some (such as college students) the net effect on post-school earnings may be positive.

- The quality of work-education programs and whether they are at the high school or postsecondary level affect their relationship to academic and other achievement. Especially important is the type of job and whether it offers challenge and opportunity for personal development.

Research and experience to date point to a need to close several knowledge gaps:

- Since combining work with education can reduce foregone earnings — the most significant cost element in schooling decisions — there is a need for research

103

on the cost-benefit implications of various patterns and sequences of schooling and work.

- For all students, but especially for low-income youths, care should be exercised to assure that incentives built into work-education programs and work schedules are devised so as to improve on the use of time and encourage school and nonschool attainments.
- While cooperative education and similar programs are often touted as especially beneficial for minorities and women, there is no reliable evidence that such programs are a better opportunity than conventional programs. They may be, but solid evidence on the matter is lacking.
- Some students benefit more from work-education programs than others, yet little is known about the study habits, motives, and social organizational correlates which may account for differences in outcome.

---

[1]Expressed as a percentage of the group who were either employed or not employed but seeking work.

[2]Prime sponsors under the Comprehensive Employment and Training Act of 1973 may continue NYC-type activities if they choose.

[3]With increased emphasis on education, training, and supportive services beginning with a Department of Labor initiative in 1970 (NYC-11), it may well be that in various areas of the country there are a number of highly effective programs. With decentalization under CETA, it has been difficult to obtain evaluative information other than the usual enrollment and placement rates.

[4]A special class is one set aside exclusively for the disadvantaged, the handicapped, or persons in similar categories.

[5]*Mainstreaming* means educating specific groups of people with special needs for life and work within or close to the normal activities of the general population. The concept promotes assistance such as translators for the deaf, back-up resource teachers for disadvantaged students, and similar services instead of segregated classes or programs for those with special needs.

[6]Hay (1969), however, found higher academic performance among

working students whose jobs were related to major field of study than among those with unrelated work.

[7]These relatively low proportions are hardly surprising, since CW-S is generally administered as a straightforward student financial assistance program, and many on-campus jobs are routine. In this and other respects, the program differs little from NYC-type programs at the high school level.

[8]For example, 68 percent of the students who chose their own jobs, but only 38 percent of those who had little or no choice, said they were "very satisfied."

[9]An exception would be purely "make-work" slots, but these are probably rare.

[10]It is often asserted that women and minority men are especially likely to benefit from cooperative program experiences. However, other than testimonials for "successful" co-op students, we have encountered no research on this important subject. The logic is clear, but evidence is lacking.

6.
Career Guidance

In the course of a normal lifetime, people develop competencies, acquire information and self-understanding, and make decisions regarding education, employment, marriage, where to live, and so forth. Much of the guidance for these decisions is obtained informally through discussions with family and friends, the media, self-exploration of interests and capacities, reading, and so forth. Even at key decision points, where one might anticipate that trained guidance personnel would be especially important, people normally rely heavily on family and friends. In a study of over 30,000 high school seniors in four states, for instance, Tillery (1973) reports that of those who considered college, the most frequently cited sources of advice about choice of college were: parents, 43 percent; counselors, 22 percent; other students, 16 percent; teachers, 10 percent; and college admissions officers, 9 percent.

Just as education is often equated with schooling, many people equate guidance with the activities of guidance counselors. In this more restricted sense, Eli Ginzberg's definition (1971, p. 4) is rather typical: "Career guidance is a process of structured intervention aimed at helping individuals to take advantage of the educational, training, and occupational opportunities that are available." Over the past quarter century, however, a number of changes have occurred in career guidance theory and practice. Early conceptions of occupational choice — which emphasized a "once-and-for-all" kind of decision — have been replaced by more comprehensive, developmental theories of career decision making. Consistent with this change, the functions of career guidance have expanded, and almost exclusive reliance on the counselor is being gradually supplemented to involve teachers in the classroom, computers, greater self-direction, career centers, and use of paraprofessionals along with specially trained guidance personnel.

Prior to the end of World War II, the job of guidance personnel was considered to be helping people match up their interests and abilities *(traits)* with the requirements of occupations *(factors)*. To this end, vocational counselors relied heavily on psychometric techniques, such as aptitude tests and interest inventories, and provided as much information as they could about occupations and education and training opportunities. The work of Ginzberg and his associates (1951) led to what Zaccaria (1970, p. 41) refers to as the "first explicitly developmental theory" of career development and choice. Work by Super and Roe in the mid-1950s and the findings of Thorndike and Hagen (1959) on the low predictive value of verbal occupational preferences confirmed the need to look at vocational behavior developmentally and to recognize changes over time both in interests and aptitudes and in the opportunities and constraints people face. More recently, increasing attention has been paid to non-decision-making needs, lifestyle preferences, and the wider domain of human development, of which career development is but one important part (Herr, 1974). This broader perspective takes into account the women's movement, cultural diversity; individual differences; opportunities implicit in advances in productivity; the interrelatedness of paid employment, unpaid work, and other life activities; developmental stages in adulthood; and growing interest in servng the needs of reentry women and mid-career changers.

Needs, Functions, and Approaches

Developmental theories of career decision-making draw attention to the antecedents of "occupational choice" as well as to subsequent change. The effects of family and culture are evident very early in a child's life, and are remarkably persistent over time. Major differences in the vocational aspirations of boys and girls, for example, are readily detected at ages 3, 4, and 5 (Kirchner and Vondracek, 1973). In a recent study, Grandy (1973) was able to account for nearly half the variation in the occupational preferences of 500 college students using only eight family background variables. As Holland (1975, p. 31) points out: "Surveys of high school and college students present a consistent picture: friends, family, schoolwork, and work experience are the most potent influences [on vocational choice], whereas counselors and tests are usually at the bottom of these listings." There is room, of course, for structured, purposeful intervention. Indeed, one argument for professional guidance and counseling is that poeple with special training and skills are in a better position than most parents and friends to enhance decision-making skills and to provide useful information and advice.[1]

Modern theories of career decision-making identify three stages in the development of young people between the ages of 5 and 18: career awareness, career exploration, and career preparation. In the first stage, the career education movement, which places considerable emphasis on the guidance function, has had greatest acceptance at the elementary school level with approaches such as field trips, modifications of the curriculum, and greater use of television and other audio-visual tools. Goals and objectives include development of problem solving and interpersonal skills, understanding of self and others, and knowledge of the kinds of work people do (McKinnon and others, 1975).

Career exploration, the second phase, takes place in a number of ways: reading, observing people at work, and hearing about their experiences. Other ways involve after-school activities, vocational and volunteer work, part-time and summer jobs, and the like. Career preparation, the third phase, refers to acquisition of knowledge and skills especially suited to a particular kind of work. Typically involved at this stage is taking a job or selecting (or being assigned to) a particular program of instruction. In addition to a number of vocational options, enrollment in a college preparatory curriculum, a decision to enter military service, and choice of a technical school or college illustrate career preparation decisions.

The traditional view of career guidance emphasizes rational, goal-oriented behavior and assumes that life satisfaction will be enhanced by (1) examining one's abilities, interests, values, and circumstances and (2) learning about kinds of work (or further education) consistent with that assessment. The traditional functions of career guidance implied by this view involve testing, administering interest inventories, and providing occupational and educational information.[1] In a national survey of 32,000 youths sponsored by the American College Testing Program in spring 1973, 75 percent of eighth-grade girls said they "would like help" with making career plans. Among eleventh graders, 79 percent gave the same response (Prediger, Roth, and Noeth, 1974, p. 99).

In 1974, an estimated 44,000 counselors worked in the schools (U.S. Bureau os Labor Statistics, 1976, p. 75). Considerably fewer worked in other settings: 7,000 employment counselors, 19,000 rehabilitation counselors, and 4,100 college career planning and placement counselors. In one national survey carried out in fall of 1966, school counselors reported spending, on average, 40 percent of their time counseling individual students, with the largest block of this time helping students with their college plans (Campbell, 1968). High school students reported seeking educational guidance, vocational guidance, and personal adjustment counseling — in that order. Asked to list the kinds of people they would go to for help with occupational plans or personal problems, 65 percent of the students named a counselor, 64 percent parents, 35 percent teachers, and 33 percent friends. No other person (for example, clergyman) was cited by more than 6 percent of the students (Campbell and others, 1968, pp. 25-26). Four out of five students reported reading occupational literature, but over a third said the kind of information they seek is not available. Two-thirds indicated that vocational counseling services were available at their school, but only one-fourth reported using such services. Seniors who had attended the same school for three or four years usually reported having had four individual conferences with counselors. If each session averaged 15 minutes, the typical student spent about one hour during high school in one-to-one counseling, with only a fraction of that time devoted to career guidance.

Guidance and counseling, especially in their traditional form, do not address all career development and decision-making needs of everyone. For example, the logic of interest measurement is to suggest occupations to people based on two rationales: (1) If a person likes the same things that people in a particular job like, the person will be satisfied with that job. (2) If people like activities similar to the activities required by a job, they will like those job activities and consequently be satisfied with their job (Cole and Hanson, 1975, p. 6). However, given sex differences in socialization — for example, women having less access to equipment and tools — and the dearth of women in many prestigious, well-paid occupations traditionally held by men, the empiricism of interest measurement becomes, in the words of Esther Diamond (1975, p. xv), "a weakness instead of a strength, impeding the path of constructive change."

There are other examples of people with special needs that are not addressed by conventional guidance practices, such as ex-prisoners, high school dropouts, the elderly, gifted individuals, and those with physical or mental impairments. Some students, furthermore, are not interested in making decisions (Crites, 1969), possibly because they feel they have no choices. Others feel uncomfortable with rational behavior. Some persons express goals (such as high income) that may be disagreeable to those in a position to offer guidance. Many students seek help in finding work, and are disappointed when career guidance programs fail to provide this service. Some individuals may not have the prerequisite verbal and other skills expected by a particular guidance program. Some youths and adults need help in grooming, exchanging information, being assertive but not aggressive, and so forth. Women re-entering the labor force may need not only information about employment and training opportunities, but also support and reassurance, help in handling family tensions, and child care services. According to Arbeiter (1976), adults are especially interested in information on jobs, careers, and education options. Whether guidance personnel can help depends on their ability to stimulate career exploration and on their precise knowledge of occupations and careers.

One unconventional guidance program was undertaken in the mid-1960s to assist ten underachievers: seven tenth and eleventh graders and three community college students, all minority group members (Allen, 1975). Each high school student was doing less than C-level work. The community college students were paid $1 per hour for classroom attendance plus a bonus each month for grades. The high school students were paid $5 per month for each A or B. A counselor met with each student once a month in problem-solving sessions based on written teacher reports. Grades immediately improved as time was devoted to studies and as parents and teachers responded positively to the change. Followed up eight years later, all of the high school students had graduated from high school, five had gone to college, and three had graduated from a four-year college.

112

Interest in a wider array of approaches to career guidance is partly a response to new theories of career development and choice, partly a reflection of the variety of needs and circumstances people face, and partly a matter of cost, efficiency, and effectiveness. One project which illustrates the variety of perceived needs in grades K through 12 is the Career Education Consortium Project, operated by the College Entrance Examination Board in cooperation with several state and local education agencies. Work is under way in the following areas: career awareness, economic literacy, development of job-seeking skills (such as resumes, letters of application, interviewing for jobs), values clarification, and individual decision making (Interview with Sidney Marland, October 21, 1976). Another project, carried out in Houston, Texas, and entitled Project EVE (Equal Vocational Education), facilitated the training of high school girls in vocational fields traditionally closed to their sex (Lerner and others, 1976). Activities included an 80-minute career-planning unit, individual counseling if desired, and support and follow-up for girls expressing an interest in possibly enrolling in a nontraditional vocational program. The project activities appear to have had an effect not only on understanding and attitudes but on actual behavior: for the first time in that school, a few girls subsequently entered traditional male vocational programs, such as automobile mechanics, air conditioning, metal trades, radio and television repair, and plumbing. By contrast, there were no girls in traditional male programs at Reagan High School, which did not have EVE activities and served as the comparison group. Moreover, attitudes and beliefs measured at two times revealed essentially no change at Sam Houston High School, but movement toward a "more traditional" point of view at Reagan.

Computer-Based Career Information Systems

Since the early 1960s, the computer has come to play an important role in career guidance. Its use has been prompted by several developments: (1) the sheer volume of occupational, education, and labor market information; (2) the greater capacity of a computer to store and retrieve such information; (3) the impersonality of the computer (many people — especially young people — feel more comfortable "talking" candidly with a computer than with a school official); and (4) unit cost reductions, bringing computer use within reach of local education and other agencies.

According to Bowlsbey (1975), five of the guidance systems developed over the decade 1964-1975 are currently operational:

1. Occupational Information Access System (OIAS), created by a consortium of agencies in Oregon;
2. Computerized Vocational Information System (CVIS), developed at Willowbrook High School in Illinois;
3. System for Interactive Guidance and Information (SIGI), developed by the Educational Testing Service;
4. Guidance Information System (GIS), created by a private firm in Massachusetts;
5. Education and Career Exploration System (ECES), a product of IBM.

Student user cost per hour ranges from $2 to $12, with most between $2 and $4. Each of the five systems is user interactive.[3] Most provide information about occupations, colleges, technical and specialized schools, military programs, and job placement, tailored to the interests and values of the user. Table 6.1, developed by Stern (1975), describes the five computer systems in operation.

Bowlsbey (1975, p. 186) cites a number of studies indicating that students like computer-based systems and use them; parents are enthusiastic about their use; students show an increase in vocational maturity subsequent to use; students gain information and engage in career exploration; and some functions can be as effectively performed by a computer system as by a counselor.

Table 6.1
Selected characteristics of five computer-based
career guidance systems

System	Information Topics and Coverage of Occupations	Localized and State as well as National Occupational Information	Accuracy and Currency	Brief Overview of Occupation Provided	Referral to Other Sources of Information	Job Search Information Available
OIAS	• Most occupational information topics covered for most occupations in Oregon and other significant occupations outside State when data available. • Coverage of post-secondary institutions limited to Oregon.	• Both State and local information about occupations and education/training. • 5-person research staff compiles information for all major labor market areas in Oregon.	• Continual review and yearly update of occupational and education-training information when new data available. • Occupational review panels to validate information.	• Has 300 word occupational brief for each occupation in file.	• Bibliography of reference materials about occupations. • Taped interviews with workers • Names of local people who can discuss occupations.	No
CVIS	• Most information topics covered for wide spectrum of occupations. • Has military information and national file of 1510 4-year colleges.	• No local or State occupational information. • National information purchased from Ferguson and Co. • Has local education, training, and apprenticeship info. for Villa Park, Illinois, other CVIS sites encouraged to obtain similar local information.	• Ferguson & Co. updates every 2 years the national occupational information in provides. • College data file updated yearly by direct mailing to admission offices.	• Provides overview.	None	• List of employers in DuPage County, Ill., who offer entry opportunities in particular occupational category.
SIGI	• Most information topics covered for] wide spectrum of occupations. • Detailed education/training info. for community college using system. • 4-year colleges described within 300 mile radius of user community college.	• No local or State occupational information but attempt to develop regional information.	• General occupation descriptions updated yearly. • Change-sensitive topics like wages and outlook updated semi-annually. • Information review and update performed by an occupational information specialist and 2 ETS Research Asst's.	• Provides brief description of job duties and tasks • User can compare 3 occupations on a single topic (e.g. wages, outlook, etc.).	• Referral to trade and professional associations.	No.
GIS	• National college data base is comprehensive; includes 2-year and 4-year colleges. • Most occupational topics covered for wide spectrum of occupations. • Data bases uneven in their comprehensiveness and quality.	• New version (GIS II) has capability to include local/state information but only national occupational information is provided by system.	• College data base updated yearly. • Occupational file updated as frequently as major sources of national information, such as Dictionary of Occupational Titles and Outlook Handbook.	• Provides overview.	• Referral to trade and professional associations. • Bibliography of reference materials about occupations.	No.
ECES (Newest Version)	• Most information topics covered for wide spectrum of occupations. • Has national file of 2-year and 4-year colleges and 1-year technical schools.	• National information culled from Occupational Outlook Handbook and from OTIS information purchased from Oklahoma. • VIEW system in Michigan will provide some State & local information.	• No verification procedures, i.e., no reconciliation of information from different sources.	• No, student must read a considerable amount of material to cover information topics for each occupation.	• One-day work internship available to student who has made tentative career choice after interacting with system.	No.

Source: Stern (1975, pp. 209-210).

Guidance Effectiveness

The findings thus far highlight two basic questions: (1) On what basis should career guidance be evaluated? (2) How effective are various approaches? Survey results such as Prediger, Roth, and Noeth (1974), showing that large numbers of students would like help in career planning, are sometimes cited as evidence of a need for more guidance personnel. While evaluation of performance should reflect needs and goals, this prescription is too simple. One study of counseling activities in a large suburban high school sheds some light on the possible implications of reducing the current ratio of students to counselors, without substantial change in how counselors spend their time (Cicourel and Kitsuse, 1963). The school had a ratio, depending on program and grade level, of 100:1 to 225:1, considerably below the 380:1 ratio in Campbell's 1966 study. The authors reported a number of highly questionable practices in assigning students to curricular options and influencing participation in school activities.

Good counseling almost surely has an effect on students, but the impact is difficult to measure. One reason is that career choice and progress upon leaving school depends on so many things, only one of which is professional career guidance or counseling. Nevertheless, Campbell (1965) followed over 700 counseled and 700 noncounseled college students, and found that the former did somewhat better in terms of educational achievment, occupational status, income, and contribution to society.

Some measures of evaluation are suggested by the objectives of guidance activities. For example, career awareness activities can be evaluated in terms of change

117

in the number of kinds of work of which people are aware. Interviewing skills, resume preparation, the logic of decision making, and job search strategies can be assessed in similar ways. To test more complicated hypotheses, such as the presumed influence of some career education activities on the acquisition of basic skills, is more difficult. The theory is that once youngsters see the career relevance for them of arithmetic and other skills, they will be motivated to learn them. Conclusive evidence on this matter, which is considered fundamental by many people in judging the worth of much of career education, is simply not available (GAO, 1976; Enderlein, n.d.).

A particularly interesting evaluative research question is posed by interest measurement in the case of women. In this case, some consequences may be valued positively, while other effects are judged to be negative. A test may confirm a sex stereotypic aspiration but also suggest new possibilities for further exploration. In this regard, three studies (Zener and Schnuelle, 1972; Nolan, 1973; and Redmond, 1972) indicate that Holland's Self-Directed Search instrument (a simulated vocational counseling device) seems to stimulate occupational exploration, especially among women.

One of the most difficult evaluative tasks is to ascertain whether career guidance activities result in better career decisions, as measured by more purposeful, considered choices of education and vocation and greater job satisfaction or success in life. The presumed effects of career guidance are clear. Greater knowledge of self and of occupations and careers should improve the match of people and jobs, contributing to the welfare of the individual and society, in part through more efficient development and allocation of human resources.

118

Three recent studies are worth noting. Each is based on longitudinal data from the National Longitudinal Study of labor market behavior, sponsored by the Department of Labor, and being carried out in cooperation with the Census Bureau by Herbert Parnes and his associates at The Ohio State University. The first two studies used national data from 5,000 men who were between the ages of 14 and 24 when first interviewed in the fall of 1966; the third study used an equal number of women the same age in 1968. A short paper-and-pencil test of occupational information was administered to each group. Although knowledge of occupations is positively correlated with scholastic aptitude and may proxy for mental ability, each study was able to control partially for scholastic aptitude, socioeconomic background, and labor market experience. Russell Hill (1977) found that knowledge of the world of work is associated with a reduction in the probability of dropping out of high school, and that the correlation is stronger among blacks than whites. Kohen and Parnes (1975) report that quite aside from socioeconomic origins and scholastic aptitude, knowledge of the world of work adds a cent or two per hour to the earnings of young men once they leave school. Mott and Moore (1976), in contrast, essentially found no effect of occupational information on the labor market success of young women.

One cannot conclude from the two studies of young men that special programs to add to occupational information can be expected to result in greater lifetime earnings. Nevertheless, the Hill study is of special interest, since if occupational information were to spur high school graduation, the payoff from investments in such knowledge diffusion would likely be substantial, indeed.

Conclusions

Our findings regarding career guidance may be summarized as follows:

- A broadened conception of career decision making, among other developments, has extended the functions and approaches of guidance personnel and the stages of the life cycle where purposeful interventions are being used.
- There is a trend away from heavy reliance on guidance counselors to more systematic, comprehensive approaches, involving paraprofessionals (including parents), career centers, computers, and curriculum reform.
- Guidance functions appear to meet important personal needs, although professional guidance services rarely have a dominant influence on career decisions.

Research and experimentation are lacking in the following areas:

- While theories of career development and decision making have been refined and extended, much remains to be learned about (1) the early acquisition of career-relevant attributes and aspirations, (2) channels of influence (especially nonschool) within subcultures, and (3) the special guidance needs of individuals not served or inadequately served (for example, adults, women, low achievers, non-college-bound).
- It is by no means clear on what basis guidance services should be evaluated. Development of performance criteria warrants attention from policy makers, practitioners, and the research community.
- The practical problems of evaluating guidance serv-

ices are understandably difficult, but these problems should not stand in the way of renewed efforts to identify short- and long-term effects. A particularly important research issue is the influence of career awareness and career exploration activities on acquisition of basic skills. Another is whether dissemination of occupational information and help with career choice influences educational attainment and eventual career satisfaction.

---

[1]One guidance strategy is not to replace the help of parents and friends but to build their capacity to be more useful (Burkhardt and others, 1977). Parents are involved in many career center activities. A modest literature exists showing how parents can foster the career development of their children. Dunn and Dunn, *How to Raise Independent and Professionally Successful Daughters* (1977) is an example.

[2]Donald Zytowski of Iowa State University (interview, July 1977), reports that an informal survey of publishers of interest inventories places the number of uses each year at about 3.5 million, including a sizable number of brief interest tests included in the Career Planning Program of American College Testing. Zytowski feels that recent economic troubles have spurred use of interest inventories in response to personal fears of making mistakes, and estimates that the volume of interest testing may have doubled in ten years, mostly in upper secondary grades and early college years.

[3]Several other systems, which do not rely on user interaction with a computer, are also in use.

7.
Learning Needs of Adults

Util recently, relatively few people have questioned the basic desirability of what Best and Stern (1976) call the "linear life plan," whereby childhood and youth are for schooling, the mid-years for paid and nonpaid employment, and old age for forced or voluntary leisure. In this section, we consider (1) the case for greater flexibility in the allocation of time over the life cycle, (2) the present pattern of adult learning activities, and (3) possible policy responses to lifelong or recurrent learning needs.

The Case for More Flexible Use of Time

The nation's system of formal education is designed essentially for children and youths. Income is transferred through the family to meet the consumption needs of young people prior to the time they are capable of earning their own living. The advantages of schooling as the major work of children and youths are clear: First, little is sacrificed in foregone earnings. Second, schooling frees parents, for a portion of the day, to perform tasks other than child rearing and childcare. Third, a great deal of learning (for example reading) is most readily accomplished at a young age.

Several developments — both empirical and conceptual — are prompting reconsideration of the way in which many Americans spend their working years, as well as the years immediately prior and subsequent thereto. One such development is extension of the life span. Another is that extended schooling has reduced total working hours in adulthood. A third development, associated with the first two, is growth in society's productive capacity, which permits greater freedom in the way people divide their time over the life cycle. While precise estimates vary, there is little question that compared with the past, men and women today have an enormous amount of time available for leisure and other nonpaid activities. One estimate (McHale, 1971) is that the typical American can look forward to a total equivalent of 27 years of discretionary time (including childhood play) compared with only eight years for our ancestors just prior to the Industrial Revolution (see Figure 7.1). A fourth development is the preference of increasing numbers of Americans (1) to work in retirement; (2) to interrupt schooling for work, service, or travel; and (3) to take time off in mid-life for personal development, schooling, or leisure.[1] A relaxation of constraints on the way in which individuals use their potentially productive years may increase total welfare by permitting freer expression of individual preferences (Thurow, 1969; Rehn, 1973; Kreps, 1976).

Figure 7.1
Estimated equivalent years spent on life activities

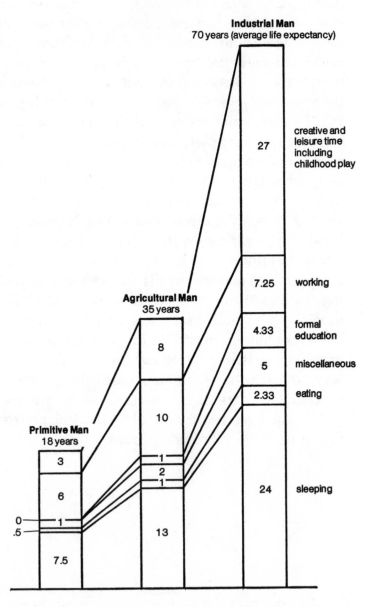

Source: McHale (1971), cited in Best and Stern (1976).

124

Best and Stern (1976) argue that recurrent economic problems of less-than-full employment have drawn tight lines around school and work, making it difficult for youths to combine school and work effectively, for adults to take time off from full-time work, and for older men and women to continue to work or go to school. From this point of view, child labor laws and retirement provisions, although beneficial in many respects, have constrained the activities of youths and elderly persons.

To Best and Stern and other researchers, a supportive stance toward recurrent or lifelong education would not only benefit individuals but others in society as well by (1) enabling youths to use nonschool time to better advantage, (2) avoiding some unproductive idleness of adults during recessions, and (3) helping meet needs which tend to be ignored in the marketplace.

Adult Learning Today

In 1969, 1972, and 1975, surveys of part-time adult education activities have been conducted through special supplements to the Monthly Current Population Survey (CPS). Each survey sought information from those persons 17 years of age and older who were not enrolled in a school or college on a regular basis. All three CPS estimates reveal a rather significant increase in part-time adult learning activities in the year preceding each survey: about 13 million took one or more courses in 1969; participation increased to 15.7 million in 1972, and to 17.1 million in 1975 (Froomkin and Wolfson, 1977). Adults take courses from a variety of sources and for a variety of reasons (see Table 7.1). In the 1972 survey, nearly half of all participants took courses offered by public schools and colleges. Over half cited a job or vocational purpose; only 5 percent said their reason was social-recreational.

The courses offered by community colleges, adult high schools, and four-year colleges and universities are reasonably well known. The same is not true of the education and training activities of employers.

A recent Conference Board study (Lusterman, 1977), however, has partly filled this information gap. In 1975, with help from the Carnegie Corporation and the Rockefeller Brothers Fund, the Conference Board surveyed a sample of 610 companies with 500 or more employees. Firms of such size account for approximately half of total private employment in the country. The survey asked about courses (as distinguished from on-the-job training from supervisors and fellow workers or simple observation, also prevalent forms of informal learning). Altogether, the Conference board survey revealed that private industry spent about $2 billion on organized instruction in 1975, with over three-fourths of this spent in-house as opposed to outside the company. Large firms were more inclined to provide courses than smaller companies. Only 1 percent of the training was in basic or remedial subjects. Over a third involved management development or supervision. Three-fifths was in a variety of other functional or technical areas.

The CPS Supplement reveals that in about half the cases, adult participants themselves paid the cost of taking courses (Froomkin and Wolfson, 1977, pp. 77-78). In another 20 percent of the cases, costs were picked up by employers. Public organizations were a heavy contributor to costs in the case of persons with less than a high school education, especially those 25 to 34 years of age.

Table 7.1

Participation in adult courses by sponsor and reason, 1972

	Percent of total
Sponsor	
Public grade or high school	13
Two-year college or vocational school	15
Private vocational, technical or business school	8
Four-year college or university	20
Employer	15
Community organization	11
Labor organization or professional association	5
Tutor, private instructor	5
Hospital	a/
Other	8
Total	100
Reason	
General information	14
Job advancement	40
Get new job	11
Community action	2
Personal-family	21
Social-recreational	5
Other	7
Total	100

a/Less than .5 percent

Source: U.S. National Center for Education Statistics (1976).

One reason for the diversity of sponsors of adult education is the lack of across-the-board public subsidies for adult learning. An important exception is the Basic Educational Opportunity Grant program, which is need based and available to persons enrolled at least half time in postsecondary educational programs. By and large, however, the remainder of federal-state financial support of postsecondary education has taken the form of institution or program subsidies or of student aid administered by a select range of institutions. This pattern has served rather well the learning needs of youths as well as of many older adults who seek existing educational offerings of such institutions. Beyond such offerings, however, public policy has been largely neutral.

The few public provisions for adult education are noteworthy, in that they indicate social priorities of public support. The GI Bill, for example, provides public funds to assist veterans in their readjustment to civilian life. Courses for registered apprentices and manpower programs are other examples. Since the early 1960s, manpower training and other services have been provided to persons who are unemployed or underemployed, with special emphasis on those who are disadvantaged by low income, race, previous schooling, age, or a disabling condition.[2] Four other programs receive federal assistance on a substantial scale: the Work Incentive (WIN) Program is targeted to employable welfare recipients; the $80 million per year Adult Basic Education Program provides funds through the states to local school districts and other agencies for basic literary training; the Vocational Education Act of 1963, as amended, provides basic grants to states to

128

serve both youths and adults; and well over $1 billion per year is spent on two programs of vocational rehabilitation, providing education, training, health, and other services for disabled adults (including veterans) with vocational potential.

Two fundamental criteria determine whether public support is warranted for a particular program of adult education: (1) type of education (for example, basic and vocational skills), and (2) clientele needs and resources (for example, those whose careers were affected by other governmental action and persons with low income or who face obstacles to employment). Public financial assistance has combined institutional support of types of education as well as dollar payments to persons who seek such education. Of great concern is the fact that participation of adults in part-time education is positively correlated with prior level of formal schooling; many had hoped that nonformed education would have an equalizing effect, giving adults who were by-passed as youths a chance to acquire additional schooling; many had hoped that nonformal education households with incomes below $5,000 per year were 23 percent of adult population, but accounted for only 11 percent of adult education enrollees. However, when measured by hours of participation in adult education activities, these 23 percent accounted for over 20 percent of the total hours taken that year. Thus, the allocation of resources to adult learning is much more equal than once believed (Froomkin and Wolfson, 1977, pp. 6, 12) and more egalitarian than higher education in general.

The absence of widespread public financing is only one barrier to adult learning. Others include the relevance of existing education programs to adult learning needs and the style, pace, location, and scheduling of instructional offerings. Which institutions are best prepared to offer services to adults? Should public schools, colleges, community organizations, or proprietary schools be encouraged or relied on to meet the education and training needs of persons who are no longer regular students? Should all types of education be subsidized, or only some? What form should subsidies take: financial aid to adults for education and training purposes? to programs or institutions? or some combination of the two?

Some insight may be gained by examining the capacity, interest, and responsiveness of existing institutions to adult needs for occupational skills. When it comes to occupational training below the baccalaureate level, comprehensive community colleges often have an advantage over specialty schools in the case of (1) adults who wish to explore options (for instance, women reentering the work force); (2) individuals who seek something in addition to occupational preparation; and (3) those who aspire to occupations where the preparation of choice involves work in the social, behavioral, or physical sciences (for instance, police work), or in other content areas which traditionally have been taught in colleges and universities. Non-collegiate institutions — either public or private — are better equipped to serve students with clearly defined goals where a short, intensive program constitutes ideal preparation. Of course, there are many exceptions to these generalizations, and states vary in their traditions and in the kinds of institutions they rely on to offer various programs.

Meeting the needs of unemployed adults illustrates

the importance of the intensity and duration of educational program experiences. Most clients of the manpower training system are young and/or female, have spotty employment records, and few skills. The vast majority have not completed high school. Local manpower program officials often must arrange supportive services and pay training allowances, and they are thus eager to place clients in training programs which are quite intensive and short. They also seek institutions which admit students at many times (or continually) during the year. Otherwise, they have to arrange temporary work experience or other assignments which place clients in a "holding pattern." "Open-entry, open-exit" programming for the unemployed has been one of the major accomplishments of manpower programs to date. It works especially well in a number of clerical areas where skill development requires a lot of practice. Curricular components have been carefully developed, and students can work to develop their skills as many hours per day as they like. This approach to adult training is often preferred by local manpower officials, despite their often having to pay the full cost of instruction. The common alternative is the public institution with "collegiate" style and pace, which may be ideal for many young adults and reentering women who do not face severe economic pressures but is often not congruent with the needs and desires of manpower officials and their clients.

It is by no means clear how the nation should proceed to expand and strengthen education for adults. At least three possibilities are under discussion:

1. Additional categorical programs to assist categories of adults or to support high-priority types of education;

2. Tax incentive to encourage employers or individual taxpayers to support continued learning in adulthood;
3. Revision of student financial aid programs to provide everyone with an entitlement to a certain quantity of education or related services.

Each approach has different implications for the kinds of students whose education is encouraged, for costs, for education and training institutions, and for the nature and value of adult learning that would likely occur. Each approach is also affected by beliefs about the purposes of adult learning, who benefits, who should pay, and who should be responsible for deciding who learns what. There are, of course, combinations of the three approaches. Possible expansion of student financial aid programs, for example, calls for decisions on eligible providers, purposes, and types of instruction. Since tax incentives have little or no effect on people without taxable income, a continued combination of the first two approaches seems sensible.

Four types of education and their corresponding clientele illustrate the complexity involved in choosing mechanisms of financial support[6] for activities encompassed by the lifelong learning provisions (Mondale Act) of the Education Amendments of 1976.

(1) In the case of parent education, it may well be that instruction is most appropriately provided at or near the time individuals become parents.[3] Child-care centers, Head Start classes, and other schools providing services to children may be the ideal service providers, leading to argument for program support through institutions serving children. On the other hand, many community colleges are equipped to provide such instruction, and some four-year colleges may have the capacity and interest as an extension of their traditional programs of

teacher preparation. Regardless of provider, tax incentives for individuals seeking parent education may not be an effective or efficient financing mechanism because too much revenue would be lost on those who now pay for such education privately, and many interested parents who lack taxable income (such as single parents) would not have an incentive to enroll.

(2) Another type of education identified in the Mondale bill is preretirement and other education for the elderly. Several educational programs initiated under the Older Americans Act of 1965 are specifically designed to respond to the special needs of senior citizens: financial management (wills and trusts); diet, health, and safety; use of community resources; intellectual stimulation; political action around special needs; speech training following strokes; handling hearing problems; and so forth. Human decency may prompt additional public concern for education of senior citizens; social benefits (such as reducing the need for nursing homes or institutional care) will encourage public support. However, those who advocate a basic entitlement approach to lifelong learning worry that some older Americans may have used up their financial entitlement earlier in life.

(3) Adult education for voluntary action is a third kind of education.[4] Voluntary action is widespread and has several purposes. From supplements to the monthly Current Population Survey in October 1965 and again in April 1974, we know that volunteer work has increased rather dramatically. In 1965, 18 percent of the population 14 years of age and older (24 million people) reported some volunteer work in the year preceding the survey (ACTION, 1975). The 1974 survey revealed that 24 percent (37 million) volunteered during

that year. Of those performing volunteer work during the survey weeks, average weekly hours increased from 5.3 to 9 hours.

Who benefits from voluntary service? The answer to this question will help explain incentives for adult learning in this area and the argument for public support. Altruistic and religious impulses, better schooling and health, higher property values, a more pleasant environment, social reforms, and maintaining or developing marketable skills are several reasons people volunteer. Recent advances in human capital and choice theory (see Becker, 1965), applied to nonmarket sectors such as the home, are beginning to help explain the level and composition of volunteer work. Using questionnaire data from 300 respondents originally reported by Ginzberg in *Life Styles of Educated Women* (1966), Mueller (1975) has uncovered several interesting relationships. Religion, place of residence (rural, urban), and the skill-building and job-search aspects of volunteer work are related systematically to hours spent in volunteer work.[5] Hence, there are indirect monetary benefits for at least some kinds of volunteer action.

Most volunteer activities involve collective benefits: for example, being a scout leader benefits one's child as well as others; teaching a Sunday school class benefits all who participate; staffing a recycling center saves society's resources. Such goods and services, by their nature, would be inadequately provided if left exclusively to the market. Thus, the absence of remuneration for volunteer service should not lead to the conclusion that such activities are unimportant.

There are, of course, alternatives to voluntary action in responding to many collective needs (with the exception of certain religious and political actions). The National Organization for Women (NOW) distinguishes between service-oriented volunteer work and change-directed volunteerism, urging its members to use their volunteer power to advance the interests of women along lines of greater economic independence and decision-making power. NOW is critical of service-oriented volunteerism, which reinforces stereotypes, encourages maintenance of the status quo, relieves governments of some of their responsibilities, and takes paid jobs away from others who have a just claim on income because of the socially useful services they provide.

There are a number of examples where voluntary action — either service- or change-directed — is enhanced by adult education and training. In the area of political reform and participation, for example, society has an interest in providing opportunities to learn about effective political action, since the quality of political decision making benefits all who are touched by it. A Home Visitor Project in Pittsburgh, Pennsylvania, funded under the Foster Grandparents Program, illustrates the role of training in a service-oriented effort (Bowles, 1976). Foster grandparents visit the homes of developmentally disabled children of preschool age and help with therapy for the child; assist parents in early infant stimulation; support parents and siblings in building warm, positive relationships with the exceptional child; and offer temporary respite for parents. The Western Psychiatric Institute provides preservice training and once-a-week in-service training in child development, family therapy, and communication skills. Another example is a course offered by Cuyahoga Community College to participants in ACTION's

Retired Senior Volunteer Program (RSVP). The course includes (1) definitions, history, trends, and issues in volunteerism; (2) information on health, education, and social services in the Cleveland area; (3) the helping relationship; (4) application of the helping relationship with different populations; (5) communication skills; (6) service on policy-making boards and committees; and (7) the volunteer role (Bowles, 1976, p. 86).

(4) Finally, there is adult education and training to secure, maintain, or progress in paid employment. Several existing categorical programs provide financial support for groups of adults who experience special difficulties: Department of Labor employment and training programs, vocational rehabilitation, the GI Bill, and the WIN program. Another group with special needs — but generally ineligible for financial assistance for education — is displaced homemakers, estimated to number about 2 million a year. Such persons are typically divorced women without dependent children. Most widows receive Social Security survivor's insurance. Many divorced women, in contrast, have little or no past work experience, and because their children have grown to adulthood, they are generally ineligible for aid to families with dependent children (AFDC). Such persons would be especially likely to benefit from an entitlement program.

The vast bulk of adults who would be reached by an entitlement scheme or a revision in the tax laws would be persons now employed who seek education to maintain, advance in, or change their line of paid work. Educational benefits provided by employers or bargained for collectively are widespread (O'Meara, 1970) but could be extended and supported on a broader scale. An important question in both the United States and abroad (Levine, 1975; Von Moltke, 1976) concerns the reasons educational leaves of absence (ELA) are not used as much as they might be.[6] The National Institute of Education is sponsoring research on this topic to seek ways to link ELAs to periods of layoff, thus maintaining and extending skills during business recessions, especially among those who have skills that are becoming less valuable with the passage of time. Another way of encouraging life-long learning would be to extend tax credits to individuals or employers for money spent on education. This could be done across the board or restricted to needed skills in short supply.

Conclusions

- A disjuncture exists between how individuals want or need to use their potentially productive years and institutionalized constraints on the use of time. Lifting of unnecessary constraints on flexible use of time would very likely raise individual satisfaction and might lessen certain social problems.
- Beyond regular schooling, the number of participants in part-time adult learning activities has increased over time. Great variation exists in (1) sponsoring institution, (2) the purpose for participation, and (3) methods of finance. About half of adult course work is for vocational or job purposes. A small amount is for social/recreational reasons.
- Aside from the regular offerings of public schools and colleges, widespread public financial support of adult learning is largely limited to basic literacy training, vocational skill development, and the educational needs of groups who face special difficulties in the labor market.

- Public finance is only one of several barriers to expansion in adult learning. The nature of instruction, the institutional setting, calendar schedules, and the time and place of instruction are others.
- Public policy issues concerning the financing of adult learning include (1) tax policy, (2) student financial aid and entitlement plans, and (3) categorical programs for specific types of education and clientele.
- Private incentives for adult learning may be weak in areas such as voluntary action, but social benefits may be high. Whether the learner has a low or high income, whether adult learning is likely to add to a person's income, and whether the learner works for pay — these and other factors must be considered in evaluating the impact of alternative financing schemes.
- Entitlement plans have the greatest potential for expansion of adult learning, especially if many types of education and a wide array of services are declared eligible for support.

The following research needs, if met, would contribute to the resolution of policy issues.

- The information requirements for lifelong learning opportunities are great. Further experimentation along the lines of the New York Higher Education Library Advisory Service (HELAS) warrant support.
- There are probably latent adult learning needs, especially in areas unconnected to the labor market, that have not been researched. Special attention should be given to education for parents, the elderly, volunteers, migrants, and consumers.
- Alternative financing possibilities for lifelong learning deserve special attention to assess their likely impact

on existing financial arrangements, employers, individuals and families, and taxpayers.

• Little is known about the tax incentives and other supports that might encourage employers and workers to add flexibility to the employment relationship by encouraging educational leaves of absence, tuition aid, and training at the workplace. A particularly fruitful area of study is how to cushion layoffs and turn idle time during recessions to the advantage of employers and employees.

• Experiments are needed to ascertain the responsiveness of adults to support of further learning in areas such as part-time training and employment for adults in working with young people after school, education for parents of handicapped children, guaranteed "drawing rights" for young adults who are uncertain of their plans or who expect to combine work at home with later paid employment.

---

[1]Trends supporting this observation include growing participation of adults in further education; substantial increases since 1940 in vacation time and paid holidays; declining labor force participation of adult men in their fifties and early sixties; and increased participation of youths and adult women in work outside the home.

[2]Manpower programs are discussed in some detail in Section 8.

[3]Cyril Houle (1974, p. 444) suggests that "any specific kind of learning is most effectively undertaken when the time for it has come" (cited in Kurland, 1976). It may be argued that much of what is now taught to youths would be more appropriately provided at later points in life.

[4]Smith (1974, p. 111) uses the term *voluntary action* to refer to "those kinds of human activity, whether individual or collective (i.e., performed by groups), that are performed primarily for reasons other than (a) the expectation of direct remuneration (pay, profits, etc.) (b) the coercion of law, custom, physical force, economic threats, or other socio-political force, or (c) the compulsion of physiological need."

[5]Mueller calls attention to recent findings by Mincer and Polachek (1974) that market skills depreciate while women are absent from the labor force. They place the depreciation rate as high as 4.3 percent per year for

college-educated women.

⁶The term ELA generally includes educational leaves, paid educational leaves, and tuition-aid plans.

8.
Employment and Training Programs

During fiscal year 1976, the nation's outlays for unemployment compensation to assist jobless workers and their families amounted to more than $18 billion (U.S. President, 1977, p. 63). An additional $5 billion was budgeted through the Department of Labor to provide training, public service jobs, work experience, supportive services, and income support to help unemployed and underemployed youths and adults increase their employability and earned income. Employability is not strictly a personal matter of skills, experience, and geographic location. The experience of World War II, which drove the nation's unemployment rate to 1 percent of the work force, leaves little doubt that employability is importantly related to the level and pattern of demand for labor services. The reason for drawing attention to this fact is that policy discussions of manpower services and public service jobs necessarily involve macroeconomic policies and income maintenance programs, since possible trade-offs are quickly evident. In this section we consider experience to date with federally sponsored manpower training efforts. We consider three questions:

1. What are the individual and social goals of manpower training programs?

141

2. What impact have manpower programs had on individuals with regard to labor force participation, rate of pay, employment stability, and so forth?
3. What social contributions if any, have such programs made — for example to reduce overall unemployment, poverty, and welfare dependency?

History

Prior to 1960, little was done to assist unemployed or underemployed adults find suitable employment.[1] A depressed-areas bill was twice veto_d by President Eisenhower before it became the Area Redevelopment Act of 1961, which authorized retraining of the unemployed in areas with substantial unemployment. The Manpower Development and Training Act (MDTA) was passed in March 1962, in the midst of considerable national concern that automation and technological change was resulting in a great deal of "structural" unemployment characterized by a disjuncture between the pattern of job vacancies and the location and skill of job seekers. Enrollments under MDTA typically involved selection and referral of trainees from local Employment Service offices to class-size projects run by local vocational training institutions. The Employment Service helped identify shortage occupations and handled the payment of stipends. Training was provided in skills centers, area vocational/technical institutes, and similar facilities.

Unemployment among adults fell rapidly in 1963 and 1964, in response to an upsurge in economic activity. The civil rights movement and the War on Poverty soon redirected MDTA to special clientele. Youths were emphasized in 1963; the poor and minorities were added considerations in 1964. Senator Hubert Humphrey's youth program proposals were reflected in the Economic Opportunity Act of 1964. The Neighborhood Youth Corps provided work experience for in-school and out-of-school youths. The Job Corps, a descendant of the Civilian Conservation Corps, provided training and other services in residential settings. Other programs were developed in quick succession, usually with reallocation under MDTA and earlier budgetary authorizations. A Work Experience and Training Program for potentially employable welfare recipients became the Work Incentive (WIN) Program with amendments to the Social Security Act in 1967. Operation Mainstream was designed to assist older Americans in rural areas. Public Service Careers provided opportunities for paraprofessional work in teaching and social service. In 1968, the National Alliance of Businessmen (NAB) was established, and federal assistance was provided to hire and train the disadvantaged on the job as part of NAB's Job Opportunities in the Business Sector (JOBS) program. Shortly thereafter, the Concentrated Employment Program (CEP) was established to direct resources available under the existing categorical programs to persons residing in areas of greatest need.

With the recession of 1971, an Emergency Employment Act was reluctantly signed by President Nixon. It provided $2.25 billion to expand local and state governmental payrolls by about 150,000 persons. The nation's approach to manpower policy shifted fundamentally in 1973. The Comprehensive Employment and Training Act (CETA) consolidated many of the categorical programs under Title I,[2] and decentralized management to units of general local government (cities, counties, and voluntary consortia of such units) with 100,000 population or more, known as *prime sponsors*.[3] States became eligible to sponsor groups of counties with less than 100,000 population — together known as the Balance-of-State.

Since 1974, when CETA went into effect, public service jobs and youth programs have expanded significantly. In May 1977, President Carter signed the Economic Stimulus Appropriations Act of 1977 (PL 95-29), obligating an additional $20.1 billion, including nearly $9.5 billion to be administered by the Employment and Training Administration of the Department of Labor. The number of public service employment slots was expanded from 275,000 to 725,000. An additional $1 billion was set aside for youth programs. The Job Corps was expanded from 22,000 to 30,000. A $250 million Skill Training Improvement Program (STIP) was funded to upgrade the quality of training for higher skilled occupations. A $120 million program entitled Help Through Industry Retraining and Employment (HIRE) was established to assist veterans, and nearly $60 million in new funds were appropriated under Title IX of the Older Americans Act.

Since 1962, changes in program emphasis and in administrative responsibility in manpower programs has coincided with (1) emphasis on civil rights and equal employment opportunity, (2) a renewed (but altered) concern for structural problems (such as urban youths) in the labor market, and (3) an emerging philosophy that every youth and adult able and willing to work should have an opportunity to do so, even if the government has to be an "employer of last resort."

Work and training programs administered by the Department of Labor involved outlays of $5.2 billion in fiscal year 1976 (see Table 8.1). The bulk of the money was spent for public service employment and for work experience under the Summer Youth Program. Aside from the Job Corps, only Title I funds are used to any extent for training — either referral to existing training programs or sponsorship of new class-size projects. With decentalization of program management responsibility to over 450 prime sponsors, the use of Title I funds for Comprehensive Manpower Services[4] is determined at local levels (or state levels in the case of small counties). Prime sponsors spent about one-third of their $1.7 billion Title I allocation on classroom training in fiscal year 1976. The rest went for on-the-job training (OJT), supportive services, work experience, and the like. We hasten to add that training funds are not used exclusively to pay for instructional services. Much of the money takes the form of allowances or stipends for trainees, which cushion the effects of joblessness while encouraging participation in training programs.

Table 8.1
New recipients and total outlays for work and training programs administered by the U.S. Department of Labor, fiscal year 1976

Program	First-time enrollments (thousands)	Outlays ($ millions)
Total	3,337	$5,235
Comprehensive Employment and Training Act		
Title I, Comprehensive Manpower Service	1,588	1,698
Title II, Transitional Public Service Employment	250	545
Title III,[a] Special Federal Programs	42	126
Title IV, Job Corps	44	181
Title VI and II,[b] Emergency Public Service Employment	500	1,872
Summer Youth Program[c]	888	459
Community Service Employment for Older Americans[d]	6	47
Work Incentive Program	20	307

[a] Includes Indian (Sec. 302) and Migrant (Sec. 303) programs.

[b] Title VI positions were extended beyond their expiration date of December 31, 1975, by an emergency supplemental appropriation which merged Title II and VI activities.

[c] Authorized under Title III, Sec. 304 of CETA. Reflects activity in fiscal year 1975.

[d] Includes Operation Mainstream (Sec. 304, Title III, CETA) and Older American Act, Title IX.

Source: U.S. Congressional Budget Office (February 1977, pp. 13, 24).

Goals

The basic purpose of manpower training programs is to remove barriers to employment for those who face special difficulties in the labor market — persons in low-income families who are unemployed or under-employed. Such programs are based on a different logic than unemployment insurance, for example, which is designed to cushion cyclical swings in jobless-ness and to aid individuals who lose their jobs for other reasons. Training is unlikely to be individually or socially efficacious if an unemployed person is likely to be recalled when economic activity picks up or has skills in demand by other employers. But if an unemployed person lives in a depressed area, lacks skills for jobs in demand, and has engaged in an extended and fruitless search for work, the unemployment problem may be "structural" (or perhaps cyclical), but not "frictional." Unemployment insurance is meant to cover only the latter two. Even then, however, training as such may not be the ideal solution. A geographic mobility allow-ance, a public service job, or some other service might meet the person's needs and desires as much as retrain-ing. Services other than training — or in conjunction with training — have the same ultimate goals: greater self-sufficiency through enhanced employability and employment opportunities.

Beyond expected impacts on individuals, manpower training programs might also be expected to affect employment and training institutions, the overall rate of unemployment, the percentage of families in poverty, and the well-being of children and of the community. Special youth programs, for instance, have at times been defended on the grounds of being good "riot insurance." The development of some 80 skills centers under MDTA has had an impact — not only on how best to train the difficult to employ, but also on instruction of clientele not eligible for DOL-sponsored training. On a larger scale, to the extent that manpower training programs help remove institutional barriers to employment of minorities and women through employer hiring and training policies, whole classes of citizens benefit.

Impact on the Individual

What impact have manpower training programs had on the employability, employment, and income of those served? Despite expenditure since the early 1960s of approximately $200 million in research funds to answer this question, the evidence is not altogether clear. Nevertheless, on the basis of his own work and that of others (Mangum, 1976; Mangum and Walsh, 1973; Olympus research Corporation, 1971), Mangum concludes that skills training under MDTA typically "brought the recipients from deep poverty to its upper levels, a significant and welcome gain but far less than the hopes and promises" (1976, p. 47). Perry and his associates (1975) reached much the same conclusion on the basis of a careful review of over 200 research and evaluation studies sponsored by the Department of Labor's Office of Research and Development. The Perry report covers not only MDTA, but nearly all of the categorical programs in existence prior to CETA, including WIN, which is still funded and administered separately. Perry and his associates organized their analysis in terms of the manpower service mix and expected short-term economic impact: (1) skill training (MDTA institutional and on-the-job training); (2) job development (NAB-JOBS, Public Service Careers, Apprenticeship Outreach Program, and Public Employment Program); (3) employability development (Opportunities Industrialization Centers, Concentrated Employment Program, WIN, and Job Corps); and (4) work experience (NYC and Operation Mainstream). The authors concluded that "manpower policy during the 1960s was heavily oriented toward disadvantaged youth, and was tilted toward income maintenance and supportive service rather than skill training . . . . [Most] program participants were not engaged in a training experience designed to maximize their individual productivity through the acquisition and development of job skills" (p. 20). Other studies (Prescott and Cooley, 1972; Cooley, McGuire, and Prescott, 1976; and Farber, 1972), and studies by Kiefer and Ashenfelter (in Ashenfelter, 1976) highlight a number of continuing conceptual and statistical difficulties in assessing impact, but Mangum's basic conclusion appears sound.

Beyond impact on individual trainees, questions arise as to the relative effectiveness of various kinds of training and related services (such as work experience) for various clientele groups under varying labor market conditions. Is work experience of greater value to youths than adults? Are women better served by on-the-job or classroom training? Is the impact the same in a slack as in a buoyant labor market? Do longer training programs have a greater impact than shorter ones? How important is placement vis-a-vis the acquisition of occupational competetencies?

The basic research problem in assessing the economic impact of training programs is knowing what would have happened in the absence of participation. One can,

149

of course, compare a person's experience prior to training with the post-training period in terms of rate of pay, labor force participation, and extent of unemployment. The difficulty, however, is that inclination to enroll and acceptance into training are influenced by the economic problems people face, which are sometimes transitory. Thus, it is not surprising that post-training earnings often exceed pre-training wages by a rather wide margin. The key question is, would earnings have rebounded as much in the absence of participation? Another important concern is whether gains for trainees are offset by reduced employment and income for persons with whom trainees compete in the labor market.[5] Sponsored on-the-job training raises particular issues of equity in selection, whether upgrading on the job would have occurred in any event, and the like. Also, the availability of on-the-job training depends on the state of the labor market and the economy.

In studying the consequences of training for the individual, two research strategies have been used. The first type applies quasi-experimental techniques and selects control groups as similar as possible to trainees but not exposed to the training program. Using survey techniques, comparisons are made in the post-training period, and differences in the labor market experiences of the two groups form the basis for an inference regarding the impact of training. Typically, comparison groups are selected from persons who apply and are accepted for training but do not enroll ("no shows") or who enroll but quickly leave ("drop-outs"). Such studies are typically restricted to a few local communities, cover one or two years, confront problems of attrition and faulty response, and are costly to conduct. The second research strategy uses program statistics supplemented by samples drawn from the Social Security Administration's One-Percent Continuous Work History Sample (CWHS). Without violating rules of confidentiality, social security data on the earnings of trainees have been compared with the pre- and post-training experiences of specially constructed comparison samples drawn from CWHS.[6] The low cost of this procedure allows researchers to look at much larger groups of trainees. But, while statistical controls for age, sex, industry, and location can be used, it is difficult to be sure that all of the underlying differences in ability, experience, and aptitudes have been taken into account. Especially troublesome is the absence of information on the highest year of school completed.

As the work of Cooley, McGuire, and Prescott (1976) and Ashenfelter (1976) make clear, most of those who enroll in MDTA-type training suffer a deterioration in earnings for a year or two prior to enrollment, as do no shows and drop-outs. Since the earnings of both rebound in the period after training — with trainees rebounding more — the important questions are: Why did some individuals not show or drop out? What, if anything, did they do to increase their employment and earnings? What would have happened to the trainees had they not completed the program? After appropriate statistical adjustments, how long might the gains of trainees (relative to the comparison group) be expected to last?

The evidence supports the following generalizations regarding economic effects of manpower programs:

- Post-training benefits have been greater in skill training than in work experience programs. Typically, training has increased annual earnings from $50 to $1,000. Improvements relative to control groups have

151

tended to evaporate in three to five years.

- The comparative effectiveness of classroom and on-the-job training is not clear. Earnings gains in the NAB-JOBS program from the late 1960s to the early 1970s imply significant effects of on-the-job training for persons fortunate enough to have been selected by employers. A small study by Sewell (1971) of rural blacks revealed superiority of on-the-job training. However, a more recent study by Cooley, McGuire and Prescott (1976, p. 80) concludes, on the basis of a comparison of earnings profiles with the CWHS, "that OJT training has a much smaller and shorter lived impact on the earnings of trainees than does institutional training."[7]

- The effect of training on labor force participation and employment stability has been greater than on rate of pay. This finding raises, once again, the issue of net employment effects and possible displacement. Wage rate is generally considered a better measure of expanded productive capacity than total earnings.

- Disadvantaged trainees have profited as much from training as those not classified as disadvantaged. (Disadvantagement was operationally defined under MDTA as low-income status without suitable employment, plus one or more of the following characteristics: school dropout, minority, under 22 years of age or over 45 years of age, or handicapped.)

- Evidence is mixed regarding effects of the duration of training and local unemployment conditions.

- Job development programs seem to have had an especially beneficial effect for minorities. Perry and others (1975, p. 142) assert: "AOP has been the single most successful manpower program beamed toward minorities, as far as short-term economic benefits are

152

concerned." However, aggregate economic activity affects impact. Between December 31, 1974, and June 30, 1976, the number of registered apprentices fell by 42,000. Blacks as a percentage of the total continued upward from 8.8 to 9.3 percent, but the absolute number declined by 2,000. Obviously, careful evaluative studies are needed in this area. Early studies of the Job Corps led to skepticism over its efficiency in helping severely disadvantaged young adults. More recent evidence points to benefits, but the cost of a year of training is quite high (Levitan and Johnson, 1975). Even if the benefit/cost ratio were less than unity, it is questionable whether a pure income transfer would be as useful in the long run.

• The out-of-school portion of the Neighborhood Youth Corps seems to have raised the earnings of participants (Borus, Brennan, and Rosen, 1970). The intermediate and long-term effects of the in-school program are less sanguine.

Noneconomic effects on participants — especially subsequent to program participation[8] — are less well understood. Only 17 of the more than 200 studies reviewed by Perry and his colleagues contained any outcome measures other than employment and earnings: self-esteem, attitudes toward work, sociability, health, and the like. By and large, participants feel good about their program experiences and feel they have been helpful. Nevertheless, some programs raise concern. The legislative function of NYC has been to encourage continuation in school. Yet, as Goldstein (1972, p. 5) notes, "Research findings on the educational impact of NYC are uniformly discouraging, suggesting that the program is badly conceived as a solution to the dropout problem. Several authors found evidence that it actually reduced the probability of high school graduation. One study (Robin, 1969) concluded that the program was not influential in reducing the dropout rate, or increasing enrollees' educational aspirations, studiousness, or scholastic achievement. Work experience distracted students who already had low grades, causing them to further reduce the minimal amount of time they devoted to their studies."

Carefully controlled research on recent NYC-type activities is simply not available. With increased emphasis on education, training, and supportive services beginning with a Department of Labor initiative in 1970 (NYC-II) it may well be that in various areas of the country there are highly effective programs. With decentralization under CETA it has been difficult to obtain evaluative information other than the usual enrollment and placement rates.

Impact on Society

Some see work and training programs for youths as a solution to both unemployment and delinquency.[9] But Paul Barton (1976) concludes (p. 1) that: "The creation of [typical] work experience arrangements which simply duplicate the kinds of jobs already available in the youth labor market as a juvenile delinquency prevention and treatment method has little basis for expectation of success." On the relationship between aggregate economic activity and juvenile delinquency, Barton (p. 1) found "no relationship or a negative one (with delinquency rising with economic activity)." Only one of several studies (Walther and Magnusson, 1970) of work-school interventions reviewed by Barton showed a reduction in juvenile delinquency, and the authors felt

154

that the quality of the job may have been the important factor. In one large, careful experiment (Elliott and Knowles, 1976) involving work experience, remedial education, and other intensive services for delinquent and predelinquent 16- to 18-year-olds, the opportunity to work made no apparent difference. However, problems in school and negative labeling by teachers bore a definite relationship to subsequent delinquent behavior. And Bachman (1971), in his longitudinal study, found that dropouts engaged in less delinquent behavior after withdrawing from school than before. Measures of juvenile delinquency and the effects on it of manpower programs leave much to be desired.

With regard to remedies for crime in general, a recent book by Lipton, Martinson, and Wilks (1975) reviews a large number of studies of the effectiveness of various correctional treatments. The reviewers conclude (p. 58): "There is evidence that the general effect of skill development programs is favorable (or at least not negative), but this evidence is less than compelling." Results seem to depend on the quality of the training, the length and intensity of prison education, the quality of work assignment, and efforts to follow up and support offenders once they leave prison. Much remains to be learned about manpower and other training programs and the circumstances under which they are successful in combatting crime and delinquency. In all likelihood, efforts to date have had neither the resources nor the attention necessary to confront such serious dimensions of the human experience.

Goldstein (1972) concluded: "Training does increase the earnings of the poor and reduce the poverty gap . . . [but] even those studies with optimistic results estimate average post-training annual earnings well below the poverty line." It is clear that manpower programs are neither a solution for all problems of unemployment nor a substitute for income maintenance. An example is the WIN program, directed specifically at AFDC recipients — employable mothers of school-age children. Insufficient work experience and support services (child care, stipends) caused more dropouts and lower placement rates than in other manpower programs. The WIN program was modified in the early 1970s to emphasize training and to award a 20 percent tax credit to first-year employers of WIN trainees, but a study of the new program (WIN-II) by Ehrenberg and Hewlett (1976, p. 231) reveals that AFDC recipients and costs decreased only if some placement service was associated with the training program.

Do manpower training programs reduce overall unemployment? Ignoring long-term effects for the moment, the answer is that any immediate influence is probably small because relatively few persons participate in work and training programs. In 1975, average monthly unemployment amounted to 7.8 million or 8.5 percent of the civilian labor force. On June 30, 1975, 168,300 CETA clients were enrolled in classroom and on-the-job training programs. Two-thirds had been unemployed prior to enrollment. Assuming this number did not work and ceased looking for work while in training, the unemployment rate would have been reduced by no more than two-tenths of a percentage point. The effect of public service jobs is somewhat clearer, especially in terms of initial impact. Yet, even here, there is considerable slippage in that local units of government substitute federally funded jobs for employment expansion from state and local funds.

Would a massive expansion of training reduce overall unemployment to some frictional minimum? If cyclical joblessness were not a problem, some improvement might be expected, but Cooley and his colleagues (1976, pp. 86-87) found that the number of persons trained as a percent of the area labor force had a small negative effect, suggesting the possibility of diminishing returns from training. However, the Cooley study is by no means definitive.

A recurring issue in discussions of manpower training programs is whether relatively more attention should be paid to the training needs of already-employed persons, most of whom are not disadvantaged by conventional definitions. In expanding firms and industries it is conceivable that inflationary pressures can be moderated and employment gains realized by upgrading existing workers to fill vacancies for somewhat higher skilled workers. In principle at least, there are possibilities of vacuum instead of displacement effects. If a legitimate vacancy cannot be filled because a qualified person is not available, upgrading an employed person to fill such a vacancy actually can result in two jobs being filled: as the worker moves up, a second vacancy is created for a lesser-skilled person.

Conclusions

The experience with manpower programs and services since the early 1960s indicates the following:

- Manpower training, work experience, remedial education, and supportive services can and do have beneficial effects for many people who face serious obstacles to stable employment.

- Manpower services can assist in raising earnings in

competitive employment, especially for deprived youths who lack job skills and adults with little significant work experience.

- Manpower training programs are not a substitute for unemployment compensation. Training makes the greatest sense for people who are willing and able to work but lack skills and have been unable to find suitable work despite an extended job search.
- Public service employment reduces dependency, adds to individual and family well-being, and permits communities to respond to pressing public needs.

The following issues require additional research and experimentation:

- Evaluative research to date has paid practically no attention to the psychological antecedents and consequences of program participation. This is a major gap in the knowledge base, and if closed it might improve selection procedures and program content.
- Meeting the needs of severely disadvantaged youths and adults, including ex-offenders, is necessarily a costly effort. In our judgment, it is worth the price to salvage lives even if the apparent economic returns do not outweigh program costs, and it may well be that the *absence* of more effective response is even more costly than the modest efforts made to date. This matter deserves additional research.
- There is room for selective experimentation to improve the relationship between the unemployment insurance system and the manpower training system. Some unemployed workers who have a strong attachment to the work force should be encouraged not only to search for work but to gain work experience and refurbish skills likely to be useful in better economic times.

158

- Reliable studies on the comparative effectiveness of classroom and on-the-job training are lacking.
- Many in-school, NYC-type programs have been less effective than hoped, as measured by gains in educational attainment. While new youth employment initiatives have been in the news lately, much remains to be learned about the structure of incentives such programs imply, the effects of stigma, the quality of work experiences, and the effects of variations in these program dimensions.
- Manpower training programs have resulted in major advances in educational programming: competency-based instruction in basic skills, more flexible school calendars, and the like. Much more needs to be learned, however, regarding how community colleges and other education and training resources can better meet the needs of unemployed youths and adults.
- In expanding labor markets, a strong case can be made to provide training to persons already employed, who with additional skills would be promoted to fill vacancies at a higher level. Experimentation is needed to see how and when this indirect strategy in reducing joblessness is most effective.

---

[1]Exceptions were temporary job creation programs of the Great Depression years and the labor exchange services provided by the U.S. Employment Service.

[2]Because of its residential and regional character, the Job Corps was maintained as a separate program (Title IV). The WIN program, authorized under the Social Security Act and operated in conjunction with local welfare departments, was also maintained.

[3]Prior to the change, the Department of Labor contracted directly with over 11,000 providers of service. Funds for classroom training were distributed through the Department of Health, Education, and Welfare to states and local education agencies.

[4]Other services authorized under Title I include development and creation of job opportunities; outreach; assessment and referral to

employment, training, or other service; orientation, counseling, education and institutional skill training; on-the-job training (OJT); payments or inducement to employers to expand job opportunities; services to individuals; allowances; supportive services such as child care; labor market information; manpower and employment services of community-based organizations; transitional public service employment; and use of Job Corps and Title III (national) program services.

[5]One may argue, of course, that even if displacement does occur — that is, if one person's employment is another person's unemployment — it may be equitable to assist those in the worse competitive position to gain a larger share of whatever job opportunities do exist.

[6]This second approach has not been particularly useful in assessing the impact of NYC-type, Job Corps, and WIN programs because the clientele have less (often no) labor market experience prior to participation.

[7]Very few small firms are in a position to provide training. Despite the fact that establishments with fewer than 100 workers account for half of total employment in the country, only 2 percent of the companies providing on-the-job training in the NAB-JOBS program had under 100 employees. Of course, large firms are generally thought to offer more primary than secondary labor-market-type jobs.

[8]While enrolled in the Job Corps, WIN, or other programs, clients often receive health services, child care, and other supportive help — in addition to a stipend or pay for work performed.

[9]Tom Wicker's remarks *(New York Times,* April 25, 1975) are typical: "In New York, robberies and assaults are often street muggings — again suggesting the link to unemployment, since muggers tend to be youths, and teenage unemployment is now running at 20.6 percent [and] more than 40 percent for black teenagers" (cited in Barton, 1976, p. 2).

160

9.
Occupational Licensure

The relationships between education and training and between education and work depend in some measure on characteristics of the labor market: employer and union practices, the services of intermediaries such as employment agencies, career ladders, child labor laws, and the like. In this section we examine one of these institutional characteristics — occupational licensure — a factor which has important implications for educators and government policy makers. In 1960, more than 7 million persons worked in licensed occupations. Between World War II and 1970, the number of licensed occupations doubled (U.S. Department of Labor, 1969, p. 1). Freedman (1976, p. 54) notes that 40 occupations are licensed in 30 or more states. Several occupations in the professional and technical areas are licensed: architects, lawyers, physicians, dentists and other health professionals, registered nurses, most therapists and health technologists and technicians, teachers, airplane pilots and other specialists in the air transportation industry, counselors, and persons in the funeral industry. Many managers are also licensed, among them contractors, bank officers, and school administrators. Other white-collar occupations include insurance agents, brokers and underwriters, stock and bond salesmen, and postmasters and mail carriers. In blue-collar and service jobs, states and localities often license dental laboratory technicians, inspectors, aircraft mechanics, automobile and heavy equipment mechanics, atomic welders, graders and sorters, bus drivers, practical nurses, barbers, childcare workers, hairdressers and cosmetologists, firemen, policemen and other law enforcement personnel.

Purposes

States are permitted by the Constitution to regulate the practice of occupations in order to protect the public health, safety, or welfare of citizens. The ostensible reason for licensure is to do just that. The usual rationale is that occupational licensure is necessary to ensure competence, or at least to reduce the risks of inadequate occupational performance to an acceptable level. The hidden reason for licensure is control of access to selected occupations, often in the interest of maintaining or increasing the earnings of occupational incumbents. Typically, licenses are available only to persons who have completed a particular program of study and, in some cases, a written or performance examination.

Consequences

Regardless of purpose or intent, occupational licensure has many consequences for the availability, quality, and prices of goods and services. Kleiner is completing a study of the implications of state licensure laws on geographic mobility. He finds that in the 40 to 50 occupations he is studying (all outside health-related fields), those in heavily licensed occupations are only half as mobile as persons in similar nonlicensed occupations.[1] In most instances, maintaining a license to practice a profession is conditioned on adherence to a set of approved practices.[2] Pfeffer (1974) reports that restrictions on entry to a licensed occupation, but not licensure per se, increases the income of occupational incumbents. Maurizi (1974), on the basis of multiple regression analysis, concluded that licensure boards, by delaying entry into a profession, often prolong a period of high incomes stemming from increases in the demand for the services of that occupation.

Issues

Occupational licensure laws and their administration are drawing increased attention, partly because of the consumer movement and desires to stem the tide of price increases. Issues include purposes, proliferation of unnecessary licensing, the functions and composition of licensing boards, testing, assurance of continued competency, reciprocity, enforcement, equity, access to occupations, and the impact of licensure on education and training institutions. These are discussed at length by Shimberg (1973, 1976). Based on his earlier work at the Educational Testing Service, a U.S. Department of Labor (1969) report on the availability and mobility of nonprofessional manpower highlighted the issue of inflation. Also at issue is the common practice of requiring successful completion of an approved education and training program for certification or licensure. Such a prerequisite obviously restricts the speed with which supply adjusts to an expansion in labor demand.

Finally, the use of occupational licensure to define the boundaries of a service for purposes of public subsidy is an issue of considerable importance. One way to define "health services" under federal and state health programs, for example, is in terms of the tasks performed by persons who are licensed. Several options are available, one of which is to license organizations (for example hospitals, nursing homes) and allow discretion in personnel policies and practices regarding use of physician's assistants, nurses, and other allied health specialists (Carlson, 1970).

Costs and Benefits of Alternatives

The establishment of boundaries as to what goods and services are subsidized — an issue not only in health services, but in child care and other areas — raises issues of alternative financing schemes and methods of social control, including their comparative costs and benefits. It is too simplistic to evaluate licensure only on the general grounds of "health and safety" and equity of access. The physicians malpractice issue is but one example. One response to this problem is to mandate periodic reexamination of competence or continuing education, but it is not certain that such provisions would have the desired effect or even that they would be as effective, efficient, and fair as alternatives, such as consumer education, peer review, hospital accountability, arbitration, or some other scheme (The Council of State Governments, 1975).

According to Louis Phillips, Director of Continuing Education at Furman University, various states require continuing education for 11 professions, ranging from physicians to real-estate brokers. Optometrists are required to take continuing education in 45 states, nursing-home administrators in 38 (Watkins, 1977, p. 8). But how should the content of continuing education be determined? Who should provide it: government agencies, professional associations, universities, or community colleges? These questions are important, because a requirement of additional education both restricts entry to occupations and, might improve the performance of those who are trained. Whether the benefits outweigh the costs cannot be answered without empirical research.

The complexity of benefit-cost calculations in the licensure area can be illustrated by an example. Animal health technician programs are growing in popularity across the country. In 1974, the California legislature passed a law to license animal health technicians. After 1979, "education in a two-year animal health technician program will be the minimal prerequisite for licensure in California" (California Postsecondary Education Commission, April 1976). This decision was prompted, in part, by pressure for a second school of veterinary medicine for the state, and by an apparent choice between more DVMs or greater reliance on technicians. Experts felt that "the proper use of technicians can reduce the veterinarian's time spent in routine procedures by as much as fifty percent" (California Postsecondary Education Commission, April 1976, p. 27).

It is uncertain whether a cost-benefit study involving follow-up of technician graduates would show favorable differential outcomes. However, in a sophisticated econometric analysis based on comprehensive survey data provided by California veterinarians, Chrysler (1976) found that for each added hour of paramedical assistance per DVM hour spent caring for animals, an additional $10 to $25 was added to the revenues of each practice — a sum considerably greater than the earnings of those who presently assist veterinarians. This example illustrates why more systemic analyses are needed for an understanding of the consequences of licensing policy decisions in all fields, including education.

Conclusions

The literature on occupational licensure warrants the following basic conclusions:

- Occupational licensure has both positive and negative effects. For some occupations, licensure no doubt serves to protect the health and safety of the public. It also encourages, especially among young people, acquisition of specific skills. At the same time, it restricts mobility, may increase prices, and closes opportunity to some persons who otherwise would be suitable candidates for positions.

- The basis for occupational licensure policy and the composition of licensing boards have come under increasing scrutiny, in part because boards in many states do not have lay members and because the bases for decisions are often arbitrary and uninformed.

- Mandatory continuing education for relicensure in several professions is an emerging concept; several states have already passed laws requiring such education.

The following gaps in knowledge inhibit more informed policy in the area of licensure:

- Little is known about the multiple, systemic impacts

of licensure decisions. Since occupational licensure is only one method of social control, careful calculation of the likely benefits and costs of alternative actions is called for. Areas that deserve immediate attention include the licensing of childcare workers, the use of licensure as a device to draw boundaries as to what is "health care" for purposes of tax and expenditure policy, and the effects of mandatory continuing education for the professions.

- Relatively underexplored are ways to strengthen the beneficial social effects of licensure while minimizing adverse impacts. In particular, equitable low-cost means should be developed for suitable candidates to qualify for licenses in nontraditional ways.

---

[1]Personal communication, December 1977.

[2]Prohibition of competitive advertising is one. While pointing out that on theoretical grounds no reliable prediction is possible as to the effect of advertising on prices, Benham (1972) found eyeglasses to be priced lower in states that allowed advertising than in states that did not.

10.
Recommendations of the Task Force

To Educators

Although it is difficult to think of anyone who is not an "educator," if one has in mind people who share knowledge and skills with others, our remarks here are directed principally to those responsible for schools and colleges — members of governing boards, college presidents, school superintendents, other administrators, faculty, teachers, and specialists such as guidance counselors. We hope that professional educators, in the years ahead, will increase their efforts to enhance the contributions which others make to the development of human potential.

The Role of Educators

The richness of the environment outside schools and colleges, and evidence that extra-school experiences are often preeminent in influencing what people derive from schooling, argue for educators to broaden their concept of their role., The Task Force recommends: *that educators seek to enhance the joint contribution of schools and families by working closely with parents on developing the reasoning and other basic skills of their children, especially in the preschool and early grades;*

168

work with community leaders and employers in development of curricula and quality work-education programs; and work with state and other agencies — including the media — to improve career guidance and related services.

Elementary and Secondary Schools

Compared with the elementary grades and higher education, little attention has been paid in recent years to the purposes and performance of secondary schools, the task of which is to foster the development of each young person's potential. All youths should develop basic life competencies as citizens, consumers, family members, and workers at home or in the labor market. The extension of adolescence and youth into the late teens and early twenties and the expected future demands for recurrent education place a heavy responsibility on schools to assist young people in developing basic skills needed for further learning at later points in their lives. The Task Force recommends: *that local school officials and teachers (1) continue to emphasize basic skills; (2) establish performance goals whenever possible; (3) provide high-quality options to traditional curricula (such as carefully conceived experiential learning opportunities); (4) avoid unnecessary compartmentalization of programs and invidious status distinctions among them; (5) seek better use of student time; (6) reduce sex stereotypes and other sources of bias; (7) employ trained guidance personnel in guidance activities; and (8) keep all students as close to the "mainstream" as possible.*

169

Colleges and Universities

Colleges and universities can enhance the relationship between education and work in a number of ways. As in the case of elementary and secondary schools, institutions of higher education not only develop manpower but are important employers and users of talent as well. The Task Force recommends: *that college and university officials (1) examine their own actions to see if they contribute to imbalances between supply and demand in labor markets; (2) where appropriate, respond to indicators of imbalance; (3) work cooperatively with secondary schools to delineate functions, reduce overlap, and assure program continuity; (4) seek to assure as much learning value as possible from College Work-Study assignments, field experiences, and internships; and (5) indicate to students, especially those firmly committed to the liberal arts or teaching, how to combine subject matter interests with the development of marketable skills.*

Adult Learning Needs

Demographic and other trends suggest that increasing numbers of adults will be returning to school — either full or part time — in the years ahead. All educational institutions with interest and ability to respond should examine, if they have not done so already, how they might meet such needs. Professional schools and research universities, such as U.C. Berkeley, UCLA, Stanford, and the University of Michigan, should continue their efforts to provide continuing education for lawyers, engineers, physicians, and others who desire it. Schools of business administration can provide

170

continuing education to middle-level managers. Community colleges, vocational/technical schools, and some high schools are in a position to assist women reentering the labor force, craft workers being groomed for supervisory positions, and the like. The Task Force recommends: *that school and college officials (1) work closely with mayors and governors to respond to the needs of adults in developing employment skills; (2) adjust calendars and adapt programs to adult clientele; (3) assist employers and professional and employee associations in solving such problems as obsolescence; (4) adjust personnel policies to make better use of practitioners in training roles; and (5) coordinate their efforts with other education and training institutions to minimize unnecessary duplication of effort.*

System-Wide Matters

Several problem areas call for increased cooperation and coordination of effort between higher education and the schools and between state officials and local education agencies. As discussed in Section 9, occupational licensure has expanded over the years, causing a "closing off" of certain pathways to selected occupations. The External Degree Program of the Regents of the University of the State of New York, in devising a nontraditional alternative — via examinations — to degrees in nursing and accounting, facilitated reform of professional credential requirements in two areas.

Additional areas of concern call for state/local or state/institution cooperation. One such area is guidance and counseling, where the extensiveness of the labor market and economies in the development and

171

utilization of educational and occupational information make collaborative arrangements highly desirable. Accurate and timely labor market information is important for school counselors and for school leaders. State labor departments should be in a position to provide education agencies with labor market information in a form usable for program planning, establishment of new programs, and for counseling students. Another area of concern is staff development. Here colleges and universities, teacher training centers, local districts, and employers can all benefit from joint action. Another area in which state/local cooperation would be fruitful involves developing closer links between education and the business and industry community. State education agencies may assign liaison persons for the sole purpose of identifying ways to make the education system more responsive to the needs of business and industry. Industry-education coordinators with experience in both education and the business world can develop the contacts and relationships that are needed to identify current and projected employment requirements. At the same time establishment of industry-education councils in strategic locations within a state can bring together industrial and education officials in an atmosphere of cooperation. The Task Force recommends: *that schools and colleges work closely with state officials (1) to develop comprehensive career guidance systems serviceable to youths and adults; (2) to assure that pre-service and in-service training of administrators, teachers, and staff specialists is responsive to the realities of the labor market and to the emerging new competencies of educators; and (3) to develop nontraditional alternatives to the acquisition of credentials in the trades and professions.*

Work-Education Programs

Cooperative education — which both develops skills and tests career interests — and other kinds of work-education programs are an important component of the general educational system. Some programs, such as College Work-Study have as their principal goal financial support — reducing the barriers to college attendance or reducing economic need, while other programs have learning goals uppermost in mind.

As pointed out in Section 5, work-education programs differ enormously in purpose, clientele, quality, and effectiveness. Further, some programs of this type are offered (or taken) for the wrong reasons — to avoid discipline problems in the classroom, to avoid unpopular subject matter, to avoid homework, and so forth. Despite these problems, the Task Force believes that work and work experience for students can be educative, and therefore recommends: *that schools and colleges (1) clearly define the purposes of work-education programs; (2) carefully select (and encourage) students to participate who can profit therefrom; (3) devote resources necessary to assure high quality; and (4) carefully link experiential learning to work in classrooms and laboratories.*

To Employers and Employee Organizations

Employers come in all shapes and sizes. Some organizations are large and technically sophisticated, such as IBM, Kodak, and Bell Laboratories. Others are small and not much affected by technological developments, at least within their own establishments, for example specialty retail stores, small trucking firms, and home building contractors. The employment needs of these varied organizations differ, making it difficult to structure advice applicable to all. Employee organizations[1] are just as diverse. And as the organizations differ, so do the individuals within them who make the decisions. Chief executive officers, supervisors, and personnel officers — all "employers" — respond differently to this role; and local officers of unions often have different views from line-and-staff officers at city, state, and national levels.

We feel, nevertheless, that major corporations, public utilities, and units of general government at all levels have a special responsibility to provide the kind of leadership which will help develop and properly utilize the nation's human resources. In the judgment of the Task Force, five areas deserve priority attention by employers and employee organizations.

Responding to Labor Market Realities

As indicated in Figure 10.1, the labor force will grow over the next 15 years differently than it did during the past 15. Women and young adults 25 to 44 years of age will account for much of the net increase in the labor force. The number of young people will remain high until the early 1980s, then decline somewhat. However, within some demographic subgroups, including blacks, the number will continue upward because of higher-than-average birth rates. While college attendance rates of high school graduates have stabilized, an abundance of young people with bachelor's degrees in teaching and the liberal arts and others with doctoral-level training may continue for some years.

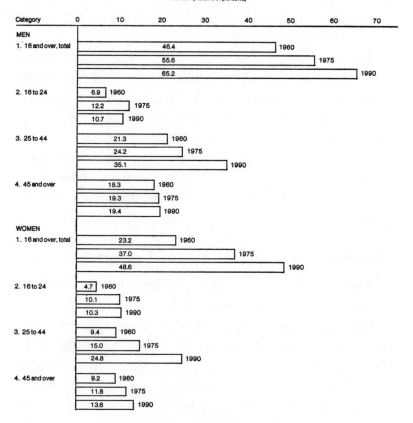

Figure 10.1
Percentage of Civilian Labor Force by Age and Sex,
1960, 1975, and 1990

Number (millions of persons)

Category								
	0	10	20	30	40	50	60	70

MEN

1. 16 and over, total — 46.4 (1960), 55.6 (1975), 65.2 (1990)

2. 16 to 24 — 6.9 (1960), 12.2 (1975), 10.7 (1990)

3. 25 to 44 — 21.3 (1960), 24.2 (1975), 35.1 (1990)

4. 45 and over — 18.3 (1960), 19.3 (1975), 19.4 (1990)

WOMEN

1. 16 and over, total — 23.2 (1960), 37.0 (1975), 48.6 (1990)

2. 16 to 24 — 4.7 (1960), 10.1 (1975), 10.3 (1990)

3. 25 to 44 — 9.4 (1960), 15.0 (1975), 24.8 (1990)

4. 45 and over — 9.2 (1960), 11.8 (1975), 13.6 (1990)

Source: Fullerton and Flaim (1976), p. 5; and U.S. President, *Employment and
Training Report of the President* (1977), p. 139.

175

Long-range corporate planning to meet human resource and production needs is increasingly important, not only because of changing demographics but also as a result of technological change, shifts in world markets, and affirmative action goals. In large enterprises, including government agencies, upgrading possibilities, motivation, and the transferability of knowledge and skill from one job to another are importantly interrelated.

For all of these reasons, the Task Force recommends: *that employers carefully plan short- and long-term responses to changes in the availability of persons entering or reentering the work force, and give special attention to restructuring jobs, adding flexibility where possible to encourage job sharing, part-time, and intermittent work, and developing ways to help those with little work experience become productive on the job.*

Cooperation with Schools and Colleges

Many students, families, and schools are relatively isolated from changes occurring in employment and in other areas of adult life. Such isolation helps no one. College faculty, for example, often have difficulty judging trends in employer hiring policies and practices and keeping abreast of changes in the content of occupations. While we would not advise schools to alter their curricula in response to short-run developments, over time the counsel of employers and former students can assist schools and colleges. Banks, local utilities, and other employers often have an interest in educational institutions beyond the issue of taxes and good schools for children in their community. Leaders in these industries are often eager to work more closely with educators. Industries hiring substantial numbers of college graduates as well as professional organizations can often be counted on to work collaboratively with teachers, professors, other specialists, and school administrators. Employers benefit from access to a better qualified work force. Schools and colleges benefit from being able to articulate their curricula with the employment needs of individuals and employers. Students benefit from career exploration, work experience, and a clear idea of the relevance of classroom work to their own career development.

We are convinced (1) that employers, schools, and all who wish to learn about work have overlapping interests and (2) that by working together more can be accomplished than by working apart. Therefore, the Task Force recommends: *that employers, employee organizations, and educators work together in ways that are mutually beneficial to learners. Employers should articulate more clearly the qualities they seek in the graduates of schools and colleges, and assist schools and colleges by providing part-time student job opportunities, faculty-staff development programs (for instance in the summer), and assistance with student guidance. Educators should work to see that learners acquire and practice skills of value in employment.*

Meeting Employment Needs of Youths

For many youths, finding secure and productive employment is a serious problem. Outright unemployment or absence from school and the work force is especially serious among minorities, particularly those who have little education, spotty work records, and who live in poverty neighborhoods in large cities.

The magnitude of youth unemployment is apparent; causes and solutions are somewhat less clear, except that the size of the youth cohort itself and protracted recessions in 1970-71 and 1974-76 are importantly implicated. Inadequate socialization — not wholly the responsibility of schools and colleges — is also a factor. We suspect, based on evidence reviewed in Section 3, that unrealistically high occupational and wage ,expectations are not an important factor in the persistent, high differential between youth and adult unemployment rates. Preferences for part-time and temporary work, however, probably are — at least for youths still in school.

Educators can contribute to the employability of students by improving the performance of schools and colleges. Employers can do the same by making the early work experiences of young people as beneficial as possible. "Youth jobs" can help youths explore aptitudes, abilities, and interests, and learn those habits of mind and character that are important in nearly all employment relationships: perseverance and hard work, care and safety, punctuality, getting along with others, and so forth. The Task Force recommends: *that employers and employee organizations (1) work closely with educators through Community Education-Work Councils and with employment and training officials to assist in developing job opportunities and carefully designed work-education programs to encourage close ties between work in school and work outside and (2) support efforts to test the feasibility of federal-state payment of the nonwage, social security costs of employing youths in general (see recommendations to government policy makers).*

Facilitating Maximum Freedom of Individual Choice

Workers, employers, and the public have an interest in the development and productive utilization of human talents. Morale problems, job dissatisfaction, reduced productivity, and other problems can be lessened by recurrent opportunities to extend established skills and learn new ones. In earlier times, continuing and recurrent education, taking time out from education for work and travel, and devoting instructional resource to meet the retirement and service needs of older Americans were viewed as unaffordable luxuries. Today, things are different. People are living longer and staying productive longer. For many young people, it would be wise to postpone a part of their formal education until later in life — given the rapidity of change in occupational employment possibilities. Thus, the Task Force recommends: *that employers and employee organizations reevaluate their policies and strive to develop greater flexibility in hiring policies, work schedules, vacation periods, job security rules, and in tuition and other fringe benefits, so as to facilitate continuing and recurrent education of their employees.*

Education and Training at Work

A recent survey conducted by The Conference Board (Lusterman, 1977) documents the substantial amount of organized instruction provided by companies, especially those with large numbers of employees. Firms with 500 or more employees — which, in the aggregate, account for about half of total employment in the U.S. — spent $2 billion and reached about 4 million employees in 1975. Additional millions of workers no doubt learn a great deal informally on the job, through practice, observation, and informal instruction. The Task Force recommends: *that employers and employee associations work together to develop greater lifelong learning opportunities at work. Two areas deserve special attention: (1) the needs of scientists, engineers, and teachers who often suffer because of technological obsolescence and (2) the need to maintain, extend, or redirect the careers of workers on layoff so that they are prepared to take on new or old roles in better economic times.*

To Government Policy Makers

Public policy toward education and employment involves all levels of government. Schooling is principally a state and local responsibility, with local support critically important in grades K through 12 and state support predominant in public higher education (except for community colleges in some states). Employment and manpower policies, on the other hand, involve overall economic policy where the federal government is preeminent. In many areas — such as educational reform, removing financial barriers to postsecondary education, and smoothing the transition of youths from school to work — all levels of government are significantly involved.

Problems of Youths in the Labor Market

Unemployment among out-of-school youths, especially in urban poverty areas, is a serious problem, especially when the economy is operating at less than full capacity. It will be difficult to reduce the nation's unemployment rate to 4.5 or 5.5 percent unless a way is found to narrow the gap between youth and adult unemployment rates.[2] More jobs will help, and President Carter's signing of the Youth Employment and Demonstration Projects Act in August 1977 represents an important step in this direction. Improvements in the quality of schooling, in guidance and counseling, and in job placement and follow-up should also help reduce the youth unemployment differential. As indicated in Section 3, evidence is mixed as to the importance of minimum wage laws and child labor standards for joblessness among young people.

Regardless of causes of youth unemployment, its reduction almost surely depends on several actions. Most important is the creation of jobs through general expansion in the economy and specifically targeted public service jobs. We recognize that under the Comprehensive Employment and Training Act (CETA) and other legislation, it is possible to use federal funds to offset costs of employing youths whose productivity is below the minimum wage. We support such use of federal funds, and urge experimentation with additional ways of reducing the net cost of hiring youths under age 21. Rather than advocating a youth minimum wage, we would suggest experiments wherein government revenues are used to pay social security taxes for those under age 21. Such an approach would maintain the integrity of the minimum wage, but at the same time recognize the employment needs of youths whose productivity is low or uncertain. Because of recent changes in social security legislation that call for a significant increase in transfer payments from young people in the work force to retired adults or their beneficiaries, we suggest that such experiments involve public financing of the employee and employer portions of social security taxes on work performed by individuals under age 21.

Beyond actions now under way, the Task Force recommends: *that the federal government undertake a series of experiments in selected states and localities to ascertain the effect of subsidizing a portion of the nonwage costs associated with employing persons under 21 years of age.*

Manpower Forecasting

Currently, responsibility for forecasts of supply and demand in markets for highly trained manpower is split among several federal agencies, including the Bureau of Labor Statistics, the National Science Foundation, and the National Center for Education Statistics. These agencies should be encouraged and given the resources to do a better job. One means of improvement would be to concentrate on occupations where forecasts have validity and margins of error are relatively small (such as public school teaching). Another is to eschew straight-line extrapolation of past trends. A third is to build adjustments into forecasting models.

An absence of timely and reliable forecasts of trends in the labor market — especially in occupations calling for lengthy, expensive training — is costly to society and to individuals. Better forecasting models would reduce such costs. In addition, better forecasts would inform policy decisions by permitting an examination of the human resource implications of government budget options. Therefore, the Task Force recommends: *that the federal government develop models to forecast manpower supply and demand, including probable adjustments to imbalances, and that special attention be given to occupations calling for costly and lengthy training.*

Support for Information, Research, Innovation and Reform

The federal government has a special role in research, which is costly and affects people in many diverse parts of the nation. Dissemination of the information resulting from research should be an important by-product of federal support, but all too often the appropriate channels of communication have not been fully utilized. In response to the need for improved communication, the Education Amendments of 1976 called for the creation of an inter-agency National Occupational Information Coordinating Committee and for better program statistics on vocational education and employment and training programs. Government agencies at all levels should follow the example of this effort, and attempt to see that information on employment, education, and service opportunities is available to everyone seeking it.

There is much that governments can do to facilitate the work of educators, guidance personnel, and others who are concerned with education, work, and service. Assisting schools and colleges to make programs accessible is one way. Providing support for staff development is another. The Task Force recommends: *that the federal government continue to support (1) the establishment of Educational Opportunity and Educational Information Centers, (2) career education reforms, (3) strengthening of guidance and counseling, (4) development of occupational information systems for states and regions, (5) reforms to enable educational institutions to be more responsive to adults, and (6) experiments in lifelong learning.*

Review of Federal Programs

We have reviewed experience with employment and training programs sponsored by the Department of Labor, and in Appendix C we describe the magnitude of present federal efforts in areas related to education, work, and service. The 1970s witnessed a substantial increase in the relative importance of income transfers from the federal treasury to individuals and to state and local units of government. In part, this reflects decisions to decentralize, wherever possible, the administration of programs to units of state and local government. The shift toward transfers also reflects growth in social security, unemployment compensation, and other payments to individuals — including, of course, substantial amounts of student financial aid.

Without questioning the wisdom of recent developments, but recognizing the important interrelationships involving levels of government and types of spending, the Task Force recommends: *that a thorough-going review be conducted as to the real and fiscal effects of the existing array of federal programs related to education and employment.*

State Policy Toward Education and Employment

States can assist in a reduction in overall unemployment while enhancing productivity, by providing start-up training to businesses expanding or relocating in a state. The states have a very important role to play in the development of career information systems, since employment and education agencies have both interest and expertise in this area. Another important policy arena for states involves delineation of functions — for example, the role of institutions providing various developmental or basic skills training for adults. State policies can also make a difference in efficient use of community resources by encouraging joint use of expensive facilities — for example high school students and adults learning together at community colleges or vocational/technical schools. States also have a role in encouraging program articulation between levels of the school system and in helping schools and colleges to expand or improve their services. And since higher education produces much of the manpower eventually employed in elementary and secondary schools, some degree of coordination in this area is an important function of state government. Finally, because state action (or inaction) facilitates or impedes action at the local level, regulations, program standards, and funding practices should obviously encourage good educational practice at the local level, or be neutral. The Task Force recommends: *that state officials carefully review policies and programs related to education and employment and, where indicated, make adjustments to improve the coordination, effectiveness, and efficiency of state activities.*

Occupational Licensure

Much of what we have learned about occupational licensure is summarized in Section 9. The number of occupations licensed in one or more states has increased dramatically since World War II, with both good and bad results. Reciprocity from state to state is a problem; different state requirements interfere with interstate mobility. Many occupations are licensed when alternative means of social control are more appropriate or efficient. Federal and state policies on health care and child care have become intertwined with occupational licensure issues. Although members of a trade or profession often stand to benefit by restricting the number of persons who can enter their occupation, there are times when the benefits of licensure probably exceed the costs. The capacity of governments to distinguish such instances from others, however, is not well developed. To improve the licensure process, the Task Force recommends: *that state officials reform their occupational licensure procedures by adding laypeople to licensure boards, conducting their business in public, having an independent agency examine the likely impact of actions contemplated, and developing alternative, non-traditional routes to credentials.*

To Students, Parents, and the General Public

Our findings regarding guidance and counseling, curricular options in the secondary schools, the market for college-educated manpower, and lifelong learning should be of interest to young people, to their parents, to adults contemplating a return to schooling or a training program, and to parent-teacher associations, women's groups, and other organizations which have a special interest in the educational system. We address our recommendations to these latter groups and to the counseling profession in hopes that this report will be of use to them in helping individuals make more informed and thoughtful choices.

Career Guidance and Choice

The education options open to young people and adults are increasing, allowing individuals to choose schools, programs, fields of study, whether to attend college, whether to return to school, and so forth. In fact, external conditions, such as economic activity and technological developments, often force change, and individuals need to be able to make well-informed choices in response to the need for change. Guidance systems are being designed for maximum self-direction, but there remains an orientation in many guidance services toward averages, norms, and past trends. For this reason alone, individuals and families need practice in making decisions for themselves. The Task Force recommends: *that young people be given assistance in exploring interests and aptitudes, in clarifying values, in learning how to use community resources, and in developing habits conducive to finding and progressing in congenial work.*

Choice of Curriculum and Extracurricular Activities

In junior and senior high schools, students, with the help of their parents, must make a number of important choices of what courses to take and what extracurricular activities to pursue. Unfortunately, what is most satisfying at the moment may not be most useful later for employment or other needs. Therefore, a broad base of general skills is always helpful — and sometimes essential — in guiding a young person toward realistic education and employment goals. The abilities to think, to express oneself in writing, and to perform mathematical operations are fundamentally important because they are needed in nearly all dimensions of life and because they serve to keep later options open. Experiences in school, government, clubs, and volunteer work can develop social awareness, leadership, and job skills. Acquisition of manual, office, or other skills can add to employability and test career interests and aptitudes. Sports — for girls as well as boys — can develop strength, agility, and confidence. The Task Force recommends: *that parent-teacher organizations and community groups sponsor study groups and workshops to assist students and parents (1) to see what can be learned through various elements of the school curriculum and through various extracurricular activities; (2) to clarify goals and values; and (3) to design plans that take account of each youngster's aptitudes, interests, and circumstances.*

Whether to Attend College

College is only one of several channels into adult life and work. Others include training in the military service, full-time employment, apprenticeship, or attending a company school, technical institute, or business college. In addition, it is increasingly possible to work, travel, or engage in public service and return to school at a later time. Many young people need a period away from school, especially if their career plans and lifestyle needs are unclear.

There are many reasons why people attend college or some other type of postsecondary institutiton, only one of which is job or career. Nevertheless, career objectives are important. The purely economic returns of a college education have fallen since the 1960s, although they remain high on the average. This does not guarantee that a college-educated individual is better off,[3] but as we discussed in Section 2, there is reason to believe that the market for new college graduates could very well improve considerably from the early 1980s to the mid-1990s, since the number of new high school graduates is expected to decrease from 1978 on. There will simply be fewer young people seeking the kinds of jobs for which youth can qualify. This means, of course, that the events of the recent past should not unduly influence the advice given to young people who will become 18 in the 1980s. The Task Force recommends: *that parents, guidance personnel, community groups, and young people (1) pay close attention to unfolding developments in the labor market that affect youths; (2) use the resources of schools, libraries, and careeer guidance centers to keep abreast of education and employment options; and (3) consider the many reasons why one may wish to pursue one or more of the many channels to adulthood.*

College Field of Study

Sharp changes in career opportunities can occur over the space of a few years in many fields calling for specialized, long-duration training. As Freeman (1976) points out, supply-demand imbalances often oscillate with large numbers of students shifting from one field of study to another as supply exceeds demand or vice versa. Because of constantly changing conditions in the job market for new college graduates, it is important for college and university personnel and for college students to be as sensitive as possible to student needs and the needs of the labor market. The Task Force recommends: *that the services of career planning and placement offices be made available to college students and that students pursue opportunities to gain work experience, and to explore aptitudes and interests, and if attracted to the liberal arts and to teaching, be especially aware of the job market, and if opportunities are limited or if one's commitment is not strong, to examine other opportunities that combine personal interests with labor market realities.*

Adult Learning Needs

As indicated in Section 7, over the next decade or two, many adults will be moving into new jobs or new career areas, and others will be returning to the work force after an extensive absence while raising children.

In Section 6, several efforts by educators and government leaders to provide educational and career information to adults were mentioned. Support systems already exist to assist some adults who seek training, retraining and assistance in finding suitable employment. Programs under the Comprehensive Employment and Training Act of 1973 serve unemployed and economically disadvantaged adults. Rehabilitation programs are available to veterans and others who need assistance because of disabilities. Many employers provide learning opportunities to at least some employees through special classes and tuition assistance. However, relatively few people take advantage of such aid.

The Task Force recommends: *(1) that adults returning to work following an absence from the labor force assess their aptitudes and interests in terms of labor market realities and assist local government agencies, such as the public library, the schools, and community groups, to develop community-oriented counseling and guidance resources for adults; and (2) that adults now at work take advantage of learning opportunities offered at work and in their communities.*

To the Research Community

Policy-oriented inquiry, while not the only purpose of research or necessarily the most important, has several distinctive requirements if it is to be done well. It should be sensitive to issues, timely, and both comprehensive in its implications and disaggregative in its understanding. Summarized below are the most important gaps in knowledge which, if closed, would contribute significantly to public policy and private decision making. Several common themes emerging from these gaps in knowledge are discussed, along with recommended steps to improve the relationship between research and the formulation of policy.

Knowledge Gaps

Within the domain of *labor market trends and adjustments*, the Task Force believes that answers to the following questions are especially important:

1. What education and employment problems are likely to emerge in the 1980s and 1990s in response to demographic trends, energy problems, and other social and technological developments?

2. What adjustments take place in response to supply-demand imbalances in labor markets for college-trained people? High priority should be given to understanding adjustments in markets which employ

large numbers of graduates or call for specialized advanced training. Better understanding is also needed of employer responses: especially job restructuring, substitution of persons with one level or type of education for another, and preferences between older, more experienced workers and those newly prepared in the same line of work. Such knowledge will assist in the development of more reliable labor market models, which should allow for wage and price effects, skill substitutability, employer responses, and changes in occupational mobility, turnover, and schooling policy.

3. What becomes of recent college graduates who are unable to obtain work in professional, managerial, or technical sales areas? How are employers responding (for instance, with job restructuring)? Do graduates continue to pursue careers requiring a college education? Which ones are successful, and why?

4. What factors influence supply-demand imbalances in the labor market? How do educational institutions, government policies and programs, and employer practices affect supply-demand imbalances?

5. Are students responding to market conditions in their choice of field of study and whether to attend graduate school? Are there qualitative changes in the academic units of colleges and universities that reflect student response to the labor market?

6. What kinds of students are most adaptable to changing labor market conditions, and what are the pecuniary and nonpecuniary factors that influence choice of fields of study and occupation?

To promote *informed decision making* for policy makers and for students and their families, the Task Force believes that the following questions deserve attention:

192

1. What aspects of the school experience enable people to adapt quickly, to maintain better health, to be more effective parents, and to engage in quarter volunteer, cooperative behavior?

2. What are the implications, if any, of declining test scores for working life?

3. How and to what extent does schooling, in conjunction with home and neighborhood, influence the amount of education people eventually obtain?

4. How do extracurricular activities affect students who pursue them? Is the amount of time spent in these activities as important as the quality of the time spent? How do parents and other family members influence what a child learns?

In the years ahead, policy deliberations, especially at the federal level, will almost certainly involve comparisons of the effectiveness (and net cost) of the options open to young people once they leave high school. This necessarily calls for a better understanding of the implications of *interruptions in schooling, public service jobs, vocational and manpower training, student aid programs, and occupational licensure.*

1. Which elements of the high school curriculum are most useful to young people, especially those who do not plan to attend college? In particular, what knowledge and skills add to values not measured in the marketplace (for example, do-it-yourself activity)? How do newer elements of curricula, such as unpaid work experience and Outward Bound type activities, affect students?

2. Do early work experiences influence goals, aspirations, and subsequent educational attainment? Are the effects more salient for girls than for boys, for

lower-class than middle-class youngsters?[4]

3. How does the "social ecology" of the school influence the nature and purposes of work-education programs at the secondary level?[5]

4. What are the implications of work-education at the postsecondary level for lost earnings, length of schooling, and economic returns?

5. What combinations and sequences of schooling, further training, and jobs are useful and beneficial? What factors influence access to preferred channels?

6. What are the individual and social consequences of skill development, both on and off the job, in terms of productivity and sharing of knowledge and skill at the workplace?

7. Under what conditions is occupational licensure beneficial? How does it affect incentives for additional education and training? Can means be developed to permit persons to obtain credentials in nontraditional ways?

In order to assist people to make more *informed choices* and to respond to their own needs, the Task Force believes that the following questions need answers:

1. Where are the important "choice points" in the human life cycle, and what channels of guidance are most effective at these points?

2. What information and advice is most helpful to college students in the liberal arts and to graduate students, whose options in the past were largely restricted to college teaching?

3. Are guidance activities responsive to the common and distinctive needs of minorities, women, reentrants to the work force, gifted youngsters, and persons with physical or mental impairments? Do guidance

counselors dampen high aspirations if standardized test scores are low? Is appropriate consideration given to experience, motivation, and individual talents?

4. How effective are modern career guidance systems in terms of acquisition of basic skills and long-term outcomes?

5. Would support and expansion of free-standing, community-based career guidance services help satisfy the career development needs of both youths and adults?

The Task Force believes that the nation's policy on *lifelong learning* will continue to evolve in the years ahead. We therefore urge research and experimentation addressed to the following questions:

1. What personal and institutional motivations and available programs and financial arrangements influence adults to pursue additional education and training of various types?

2. What individual and social benefits are derived from various types of adult learning? Here we urge experimentation with parent education, and programs for the elderly and youths with uncertain goals.

3. What can be done to prevent or retard obsolescence among people employed in highly technical fields who have been out of school for several years and to ensure maximum utilization of their potential?

4. How can colleges, universities, and other employers use the talents of young people who are unable to secure jobs as teachers?

The Consequences of Learning

Although much is known about the impact of formal

schooling on some dimensions of life — most notably personal economic well-being — less well understood, but potentially very important in the years ahead, are effects on the quality of life and on useful non-market-oriented activities. The mechanisms through which early influences are felt later in life — post-school training, self-study, income — are not altogether clear, nor do we understand why different persons are affected in different ways. The task force recommends: *that scholars and research organizations study (1) the multiple effects of schooling and work; (2) the influence of particular sequences of school and nonschool experiences; and (3) the durability of outcomes.*

Learning Outside School

The amount of schooling one receives, extent of work experience, and on-the-job training typically influence how well a person does at work, as measured by status and earnings. Little is known, however, about the direct and indirect effects on career success of family life, peer influences, television and after-school activities. Given the very imperfect understanding that now exists concerning the way in which these environmental factors influence the development of attributes important in employment, the Task Force recommends: *that scholars devote special attention (1) to the influence of qualitative dimensions of work and schooling, (2) to the separate and (joint) effects of forces outside school and the workplace, such as family, peers, and leisure-time activities, and (3) to the influence of employer policies and practices regarding training, work assignments, and promotions.*

196

Methods and Processes

Research to date has not been as helpful to decision makers as it might have been. One problem is that researchers have understandably displayed greater interest in generalizations about groups of people than the behavior of individuals; and while an understanding of aggregates depends on knowledge of typical behavior, no individual is precisely average, and the value of programs and projects depends on carefully distinguishing impacts on subsets of the population. A second problem is the lack of sufficient longitudinal research, particularly on the early labor market experiences of youths. A third problem concerns theoretical constructs and measurements and a lack of clarity about precisely what is being measured in some studies. A fourth problem is the frequent absence of multidisciplinary perspectives. Career development theories and career guidance systems, in particular, call for contributions from several disciplines, but only rarely has such collaboration taken place. A final problem is that very little policy-directed research has, in fact, been relevant to contemporary policy issues. Although it is not wise to tie all research to policy, there are ways to assist policy researchers and implementers to work together more effectively.

In light of these findings, the Task Force recommends: *that researchers and sponsors of research put greater emphasis on (1) understanding individual differences in the effects of programs and experiences; (2) longitudinal research on the influence of psychological variables and the long-term consequences of earlier experience; (3) the contributions of several*

197

disciplines to policy-related research; and (4) exchange programs whereby researchers become familiar with policy formulation and policy makers articulate their information needs to the research community.

---

[1]In addition to trade unions, this includes professional and other organizations which represent employment and related interests of their members.

[2]See Gordon (1977) and Okun (1977) for a review of target rates, given present-day policies and the demographic structure of the work force.

[3]To illustrate, in 1972 adult white males with exactly 12 years of schooling reported median money income of $10,182. The figure for white males with 16 or more years was $14,385 (Thurow, 1975, p. 68). Yet, 28 percent of the college graduates earned less than $10,182; and 21 percent of the high school group earned more than $14,385.

[4]Hill (1977) suggests that occupational information has a particularly positive effect, via highest year of school completed, on the labor market success of young black men. The need for increased options for girls, who have fewer role models in nontraditional occupations, also points to the importance of this question.

[5]Student employment need not (but easily can) be at the expense of work on basic skills. Work in "youth jobs" is not a panacea, and several studies suggest that existing incentives lead many disadvantaged students to leave school. Barton (1976) failed to show that work-education reduced juvenile deliquency. Little is known about stigma, and the way in which students and educators view many work-study programs.

Appendix A
Priority Ratings of Suggested Research, Experiments, and Policy Recommendations

Independently, and without knowledge of how others were "voting," each Task Force member was asked to identify five research items, experiments, and policy recommendations as "most important." It was not always easy to distinguish between a research item and an experiment. In general, an inquiry was classified as an *experiment* if it called for an experimental design, required the development or testing of novel activities, or implied legal modifications in order to ascertain consequences. An item was listed under *research* if it called for study and comparison but no new actions, legal changes, or other interventions in individual or social life. Suggestions to parents, students, and other potential learners were not included in the priority rankings for two reasons: (1) suggestions to individuals are often quite global and (2) families and learners vary so much that advice to one may not be appropriate to another.

The results of the priority rating are presented in Table A.1. Members of the Task Force substantially agree that there is a need:

- To improve the collective understanding of education and employment problems likely to emerge in the 1980s and 1990s.

- To know which elements of the high school curriculum are most useful to young people, especially those not planning to attend college.
- To undertake experimental and other development work in manpower forecasting, lifelong learning and its financing, career development of college students in the liberal arts, and employer initiatives in improving the links between education and employment.
- For educators to promote the joint contribution of schools, families, employers, and community groups in the education and socialization of youths.
- For educators to improve the performance of schools by continued emphasis on basic skills, establishment of performance objectives, provision of high-quality options to the traditional curriculum, avoidance of invidious distinctions between various programs, better use of student time, and by keeping all students as close to the "mainstream" as possible.
- For the federal government to continue its support of career education reforms, outreach, career guidance and occupational information systems, reforms to enable educational institutions to be more responsive to adults, and experiments in lifelong learning.

As may be seen in Table A.1, somewhat lesser agreement is evident on several other recommendations.

Table A.1
Priority Ratings of Suggestions

Item	Breneman	Freeman	Gomberg	Kerr, Chm.	Nyquist	Snider	Williams	Shea, staff

RESEARCH

R1. *Labor market adjustments to supply-demand imbalances.* What adjustments take place in response to supply-demand imbalances in labor markets, especially in markets for college-trained manpower that involve large numbers of graduates or call for specialized, advanced training? In particular, a better understanding is needed of employer responses — especially job restructuring, the substitutability of persons with different levels and types of education, and between older, more experienced workers and those newly prepared in the same line of work.

Item	Breneman	Freeman	Gomberg	Kerr, Chm.	Nyquist	Snider	Williams	Shea, staff
R1	X	X				X		

R2. *Student adaptability and choice.* What kinds of students are most adaptable and what are the pecuniary and nonpecuniary factors which condition choice of field of study and decisions to enter an occupation?

R3. *Education and employment problems to the year 2000.* What education and employment problems are likely to emerge in the 1980s and 1990s in response to demographic trends, energy problems, and social and technological developments?

Item	Breneman	Freeman	Gomberg	Kerr, Chm.	Nyquist	Snider	Williams	Shea, staff
R3	X	X	X	X	X		X	

201

Table A.1
Priority Ratings of Suggestions

Item	Breneman	Freeman	Gomberg	Kerr, Chm.	Nyquist	Snider	Williams	Shea, staff
R4. *Underemployed college graduates: permanent? For whom? If not, why not?* What is happening to recent college graduates who were unable to obtain work in professional, managerial, or technical sales areas? How are employers responding (for instance, with job restructuring)? Do graduates try to get back on the track? Which ones are successful and why?	X	X			X		X	
R5. *Field of study adjustments to job market for college graduates.* How are colleges and universities responding to student choice of field of study, and whether to attend graduate school? Which students are responding to market conditions? What qualitative changes are taking place within departments and other academic units and in the kinds of students attracted to various fields of study?			X	X				
R6. *Causes of supply-demand imbalances.* What factors influence supply-demand imbalances in labor markets? How do educational institutions, government policies and programs, and employer practices contribute to supply-demand imbalances?						X		
R7. *Systemic cost-benefit consequences of occupational licensure.* Under what conditions is occupational licensure beneficial? How does it affect incentives for additional education and training? What systemic consequences stem from decisions			X		X			X

202

Table A.1
Priority Ratings of Suggestions

Item		Breneman	Freeman	Gomberg	Kerr, Chm.	Nyquist	Snider	Williams	Shea, staff
	on licensing of childcare workers, using occupational licensure to define the boundaries of government-subsidized health care, and mandatory continuing education for selected professions?								
R8.	*Mechanisms of effects of schooling.* What is it about the school experience which enables people with more of it to adapt more quickly, to maintain better health, to be more effective parents, and which calls forth greater volunteer, cooperative behavior? How much of the overall relationship is associated with the kind of work people do and the income opportunities better jobs make possible?								X
R9.	*Test score decline: Reasons? Problem?* What are the implications, if any, of declining test scores for working life?								
R10.	*Effects of differing time budgets of students.* What difference does it make for students to spend their school and other time engaged in various activities? How do parents and other family members influence what a child learns? Is the amount of time spent in various activities as important as the quality of the time spent?								X
R11.	*High school curriculum effects.* Which elements of the high school curriculum are most useful to young people, especially those who do not plan to attend college? In particular, what knowledge and	X	X	X	X	X			X

203

Table A.1
Priority Ratings of Suggestions

Item		Breneman	Freeman	Gomberg	Kerr, Chm.	Nyquist	Snider	Williams	Shea, staff
	skills add to values not measured in the marketplace (such as do-it-yourself activity)? How do newer elements of curricula, such as unpaid work experiences and Outward Bound type activities affect students?								
R12.	*Links between work experience, aspirations, and educational attainment.* Do early work experiences influence goals and aspirations, and do such effects influence subsequent educational attainment? Are the effects more salient for girls than boys, for lower-class than middle-class youngsters?					X	X	X	
R13.	*Ecological influence on work-education programs.* How does the "social ecology" of the school influence the nature and purposes of work-education programs at the secondary level?								
R14.	*Collective bargaining influence on schools and colleges.* What are the implications of teacher unions and collective bargaining in schools and colleges for the quality of education, teacher performance, and innovations in education?				X			X	
R15.	*Effects of schooling on educational attainment.* To what extent does schooling influence the amount of education people eventually obtain? How does the school experience, in conjunction with home and neighborhood, influence educational attainments?								
R16.	*Postsecondary work education pro-*								

204

Table A.1
Priority Ratings of Suggestions

Item		Breneman	Freeman	Gomberg	Kerr, Chm.	Nyquist	Snider	Williams	Shea, staff
	grams: *Effects? Who benefits most?* What are the implications of work-education at the post-secondary level for foregone earnings, length of schooling, and economic returns? Are work-education programs especially beneficial to women and minority men?								
R17.	*Alternative channels to adulthood: Effects? Access?* What are the implications of alternative channels to adulthood and work? What combinations and sequences of schooling, further training, and jobs are useful and beneficial? Which are not? What factors influence access to preferred channels?					X			X
R18.	*Implications of youth unemployment.* What are the individual and social implications of unemployment and joblessness among various categories of youth (high school students; out-of-school 14- to 18-year-olds)?		X						
R19.	*Union, employer, and legal influences on youth unemployment.* To what extent do child labor laws, collective bargaining agreements, and employer hiring preferences and practices influence the volume and nature of youth unemployment?							X	
R20.	*Life cycle "choice points" and guidance channels.* Where are the important "choice points" in the human life cycle, and what channels can be most effectively used for guidance purposes?		X						

205

Item		Breneman	Freeman	Gomberg	Kerr, Chm.	Nyquist	Snider	Williams	Shea, staff
R21.	*Effects of modern career guidance.* How effective are the many components of modern career guidance systems, especially in terms of longer-term outcomes (such as educational attainment, career satisfaction) and acquisition of basic skills?							X	X
R22.	*Financial and other motivators of adult learning.* What personal and institutional motivational forces influence (or fail to influence) decisions of adults to pursue additional education and training of various types? How would participation be influenced by various program configurations and financial arrangements?								
R23.	*Cost-benefit analysis to rehabilitate severely disadvantaged persons.* What are the costs and benefits (individual and social) associated with necessarily costly efforts to rehabilitate severely disadvantaged youths and adults (ex-offenders, drug addicts)?								
R24.	*Comparative effectiveness of classroom and on-the-job training.* What are the individual and social consequences of skill development off the job, in terms of productivity, sharing of knowledge and skills at the workplace, and comparative efficiency vis-a-vis acquisition on the job?							X	
R25.	*Psychological influences on effectiveness of employment and training programs.* In what way do								

206

Table A.1
Priority Ratings of Suggestions

Item	Breneman	Freeman	Gomberg	Kerr, Chm.	Nyquist	Snider	Williams	Shea, staff
psychological factors (such as achievement motivation, inner-directedness) influence the effectiveness of federally sponsored employment and training programs?								

EXPERIMENTS

Item	Breneman	Freeman	Gomberg	Kerr, Chm.	Nyquist	Snider	Williams	Shea, staff
E1. *Reliable, policy useful manpower forecasting models.* Development of more reliable forecasting models of manpower supply and demand for selected, high-level occupations (such as teachers) where forecasting is credible and useful, with a view to (1) identification of likely imbalances and probable adjustments to them and (2) assessment of the human resource implications of government policies.			X		X	X		X
E2. *Model career development programs for college students in liberal arts.* Development of model programs in colleges and universities to assist liberal arts and graduate students who have uncertain career goals, or who are likely to find it difficult to enter preferred lines of work, such as college teaching. Initiatives in this area might include counseling, career exploration, labor-market-oriented course work, internships, job development and placement.			X		X	X	X	
E3. *Initiative in lifelong learning to ascertain individual and social benefits.* Benefits derived from such				X	X		X	X

207

Item	Breneman	Freeman	Gomberg	Kerr. Chm.	Nyquist	Snider	Williams	Shea, staff
activities as (1) parent education, (2) preparing older Americans for second careers in community service (for instance Foster Grandparents), and (3) offering options to youths with uncertain goals.								
E4. *Model educational programs to meet employment-related needs of adults.* Development of model programs for schools and colleges to respond to the skill development, employment needs of adults (such as reentry women; workers on layoff; out-of-school youths). Such efforts should include adaptation of calendar schedules and modifications in other practices to make opportunities more accessible and useful.	X	X	X					
E5. *Experiments in financing lifelong learning activities.* Experiments in financing lifelong learning, to determine incentive and other impacts, benefits, and costs. Such experiments might include tax credits for learners and employer, GI-bill-type credits for community service, subsidies for tuition aid, incentives for negotiated educational benefits, and subsidies for training in the workplace.	X			X		X	X	
E6. *Model programs of human resource management.* Development of model programs in human resource management, with special attention to scientists, engineers, teachers, and middle-level manag-	X						X	

208

Table A.1
Priority Ratings of Suggestions

Item		Breneman	Freeman	Gomberg	Kerr, Chm.	Nyquist	Snider	Williams	Shea, staff
	ers, but including others. Such programs might include sabbaticals, career mobility plans, preparation for mid-career change, early retirement for second careers, and constructive use of time on lay-off.								
E7.	*Employer-industry innovations in employment and training.* Employer-industry initiatives in job sharing, modification of work schedules, job redesign, buddy systems for the hard-to-employ, and mechanisms to encourage acquisition of skills on as well as off the job. Such efforts might include cooperative scheduling with schools and colleges to permit alternation of work and study within the work week.				X	X		X	X
E8.	*Higher education initiatives to revitalize faculties and utilize young professionals.* Initiatives by colleges and universities to revitalize faculties by reducing the rigidity of tenure and opening opportunities for young professionals to use their talents in such areas as teaching, post-doctoral research, working with schools and community colleges to improve reading.			X	X			X	
E9.	*Alternative credentialing procedures.* Development of procedures to acquire credentials (degrees, occupational licenses) in unconventional ways (such as licensure through open examinations), building on the experience of								

209

Table A.1
Priority Ratings of Suggestions

Item	Breneman	Freeman	Gomberg	Kerr, Chm.	Nyquist	Snider	Williams	Shea, staff
the New York Regents' External Degree Program and other initiatives over the past decade.								
E10. *Federal-state payment of selected nonwage costs of employing youths.* Without jeopardizing the job security of adults, experiments to determine the impact of federal-state payment of selected nonwage costs of employing out-of-school youths with little or no work experience.	X	X		X				
E11. *Collaborative work experience and career development efforts.* Initiatives involving students, parents, employers, schools, and community agencies to assist youths in learning about work and its expectations, to explore career opportunities, and to acquire skills, contacts, and useful work experience. Such efforts might include improved guidance activities, staff development, internship opportunities, and careful integration of learning on the job, at school, and at home.			X	X				X
E12. *Improvements in employment and training programs for economically disadvantaged youths.* Improvements in federal employment and training programs for youths, with emphasis on jobs with potential for learning and upward mobility, lessening stigma surrounding some programs for "disadvantaged" persons, and greater cooperation with		X						

210

Table A.1
Priority Ratings of Suggestions

Item	Breneman	Freeman	Gomberg	Kerr, Chm.	Nyquist	Snider	Williams	Shea, staff
community colleges and other training resources, including Community Education-Work Councils.								
E13. *Career guidance: improved practices and responsiveness to diverse needs.* Development of improved career guidance practices responsive to the common and distinctive needs of ethnic minorities, women, gifted students, persons with physical or mental disabilities, reentrants to the work force, mid-career changers, and persons nearing retirement. Improved practices should include role models, reality testing, joint programs with employers, and greater knowledge by guidance counselors of the skills needed for success in various jobs.						X		
E14. *Model career guidance strategies including community guidance centers.* Development of model career guidance strategies, involving more effective and efficient use of guidance resources (counselors, teachers, computers, career centers, libraries, community volunteers). Such efforts might include expansion of free-standing community guidance centers and state-assisted systems for providing timely information on occupational and educational opportunities.	X					X	X	X
E15. *Selected improvements in federally supported employment and training programs.* Initiatives in feder-								

Item	Breneman	Freeman	Gomberg	Kerr, Chm.	Nyquist	Snider	Williams	Shea, staff
ally supported employment and training programs, involving closer ties with the nation's unemployment insurance system, upgrading of workers in expanding sectors to increase productivity and create vacancies for employed persons, and innovative combinations (and sequences) of work experience, training, and job search.								

POLICY

The Task Force recommends:

Item	Breneman	Freeman	Gomberg	Kerr, Chm.	Nyquist	Snider	Williams	Shea, staff
P1. *Employer responsiveness to labor supply:* that employers carefully plan short- and long-term responses to changes in the availability of persons entering or re-entering the work force, and give special attention to restructuring jobs, adding flexibility where possible to encourage job sharing, part-time, and intermittent work, and developing ways to help those with little work experience become productive on the job.		X			X	X		
P2. *Employer-union-school collaboration:* that employers and employee organizations work with educators in ways that are mutually beneficial and of assistance to learners. Employers should articulate more clearly the qualities they seek in the graduates of schools and colleges, assist schools and colleges in several ways, including part-time student job opportuni-	X						X	X

212

Table A.1
Priority Ratings of Suggestions

ties, faculty-staff development programs (for instance in the summer),
and assistance with the guidance
function. Educators should work to
see that learners acquire and practice skills of significant value in employment. Both educators and employers should strive to collaborate
closely, each performing those
needed functions which they are in
the best position to perform.

P3. *Employer-union collaboration with
community education-work councils and manpower officials:* that
employers and employee organizations work closely with Community Education-Work Councils and
with local employment and training officials to assist in developing
job opportunities and carefully
designed work-education programs
to encourage close ties between
work in school and work outside.

P4. *Employer-union policies to facilitate recurrent education:* that employers and employee organizations reevaluate their policies and
strive to develop greater flexibility
in hiring policies, work schedules,
vacation periods, job security
rules, and in tuition and other
fringe benefits, so as to facilitate
continuing and recurrent education
of employees.

P5. *Educational leadership to strength-
en the contribution of agencies external to the school:* that educators
seek to enhance the joint contribu-

Item	Breneman	Freeman	Gomberg	Kerr. Chm.	Nyquist	Snider	Williams	Shea, staff
P3.				X				
P4.	X							
P5.			X	X	X	X		X

213

Table A.1
Priority Ratings of Suggestions

Item	Breneman	Freeman	Gomberg	Kerr, Chm.	Nyquist	Snider	Williams	Shea, staff
tion of schools and families by working closely with parents on developing the reasoning and other basic skills of their children, especially in the preschool and early grades; work with community leaders and employers in development of curricula and quality work-education programs; and work with state and other agencies — including the media — to improve career guidance and related services.								
P6. *Educators take steps to improve schooling:* that local school officials and teachers (1) continue to emphasize basic skills; (2) establish performance goals whenever possible; (3) provide high-quality options to traditional curricula (such as carefully conceived experiential learning opportunities); (4) avoid unnecessary compartmentalization of programs and invidious status distinctions among them; (5) seek better use of student time; (6) reduce the inhibiting effects of sex stereotypes and other sources of bias; (7) employ trained guidance personnel in guidance activities; and (8) keep all students as close to the "mainstream" as possible.	X			X	X	X	X	
P7. *College officials improve linkages between higher education and employment:* that college and university officials (1) examine their own actions to see if they contribute to imbalances between supply			X	X	X			

214

Table A.1
Priority Ratings of Suggestions

Item	Breneman	Freeman	Gomberg	Kerr, Chm.	Nyquist	Snider	Williams	Shea, staff
and demand in labor markets; (2) where appropriate, respond to indicators of imbalance; (3) work cooperatively with secondary schools to delineate functions, reduce overlap, and assure program continuity; (4) seek to assure as much learning value as possible from College Work-Study assignments, field experiences, and internships; and (5) indicate to students, especially in the liberal arts and teaching, how to combine subject matter interests with the development of marketable skills.								
P8. *Educators collaborate with others to meet efficiently the employment training needs of adults:* that school and college officials (1) work closely with mayors and governors to see how they can best respond to the needs of adults in developing employment skills; (2) adjust calendars and adapt programs to adult clientele; (3) reach out to employers, professional and other worker associations to help them solve obsolescence and other problems; (4) adjust personnel policies to make better use of practitioners in training roles; and (5) coordinate their efforts with other education and training institutions to minimize unnecessary duplication of efforts.							X	
P9. *School and college officials work to improve career guidance systems and the training of educators:* that schools and colleges (1) develop								

215

Table A.1
Priority Ratings of Suggestions

Item	Breneman	Freeman	Gomberg	Kerr. Chm.	Nyquist	Snider	Williams	Shea, staff
comprehensive career guidance systems serviceable to youths and adults; (2) assure that preservice and in-service training of administrators, teachers, and staff specialists are responsive to the realities of the labor market for teachers and to emerging new competencies of educators; and (3) develop non-traditional alternatives to the acquisition of credentials in the trades and professions.							X	
P10. *Federal support of efforts to improve education for work and career development:* that the federal government continue to support (1) the establishment of Educational Opportunity and Educational Information Centers; (2) career education reforms; (3) strengthening of guidance and counseling; (4) development of occupational information systems for states and regions; (5) reforms to enable educational institutions to be more responsive to adults; and (6) experiments in lifelong learning.	X		X	X	X		X	
P11. *Evaluation of federal programs:* that a thorough-going review be conducted as to the real and fiscal effects of the existing array of federal programs related to education and employment.								
P12. *Government officials improve occupational licensure practices:* that federal and state officials reform their occupational licensure		X	X		X		X	

216

Table A.1
Priority Ratings of Suggestions

Item	Breneman	Freeman	Gomberg	Kerr, Chm.	Nyquist	Snider	Williams	Shea, staff
procedures by adding laypeople to licensure boards, conducting their business in public, having an independent agency examine the likely impact of actions contemplated, and developing alternative nontraditional routes to credentials.								
P13. *Improve state policies and practices related to education and work:* that state officials (1) develop information systems related to educational options and occupational opportunities; (2) work to delineate functions (such as responsibility for remedial service); (3) encourage the efficient use of community resources (such as vocational training facilities); and (4) allocate categorical funds for education to encourage good educational practice (such as "mainstreaming").	X						X	
P14. *Effects of schooling and work:* that scholars and research organizations seek to learn more about (1) the multiple effects of schooling and work of various types; (2) the influences of particular sequences of experiences; and (3) the durability of outcomes.	X		X					
P15. *Joint school-nonschool impacts and the influence of qualitative dimensions of work and schooling:* that scholars devote special attention to the influence of qualitative dimensions of work and schooling and to the separate (and joint) effects of								X

217

Table A.1
Priority Ratings of Suggestions

Item		Breneman	Freeman	Gomberg	Kerr, Chm.	Nyquist	Snider	Williams	Shea, staff
	forces outside school and the workplace, such as family, peers, and leisure-time activities.								
P16.	*Selected improvements in research and policy formation:* that researchers and sponsors of research put greater emphasis on (1) understanding individual differences in the effects of programs and experiences; (2) longitudinal research when seeking to understand the influence of psychological variables and the long-term consequences of earlier experiences; (3) contributions of several disciplines to policy-related research; and (4) exchange programs whereby researchers spend time where policies are formulated and policy makers articulate their information needs to the research community.		X	X				X	

Appendix B
Four Reports on Education and Work: Areas of Agreement and Disagreement

Several reports on relationships between education and work have been published in recent years. We compare the contents of three with the analysis and recommendations in this task force study. The three are: (1) Eli Ginzberg, *The Manpower Connection: Education and Work* (1975); (2) Organization for Economic Cooperation and Development (OECD), through a task force chaired by Clark Kerr, *Education and Working Life in Modern Society* (1975); and (3) Willard Wirtz and the National Manpower Institute, *The Boundless Resource: A Prospectus for an Education-Work Policy* (1975). The latter two are products of group discussion and reflection. The Ginzberg volume, although written by a single person, relies heavily on studies carried out over the past thirty years by the Conservation of Human Resources group at Columbia University.

Synopsis of Each

While all the reports are concerned with education and work, each has a distinctive content and set of themes. The *Ginzberg* volume reflects the position of its author as chairman of the National Commission for Manpower Policy and, earlier, as a member of the National Manpower Advisory Committee. In the first part of the book, "Education," Ginzberg (1) sketches what he sees as the desirable direction of educational reform; (2) raises several questions for those in the forefront of the Career Education Movement; (3) offers a few modest proposals to improve urban education; (4) challenges the voucher system; and (5) expands his earlier work on the theory of occupational choice and on career guidance and counseling. In Part Two, "Work," Ginzberg (1) examines changes over time in the nature of work and its social-psychological importance to the individual; (2) describes major trends in manpower supply and demand; (3) analyzes proposals and experiments to restructure work, in light of European experience; (4) reviews changes in federal funding of science and related policies and their impact on highly educated manpower; (5) discusses the significance of defense manpower policies; (6) analyzes the position of blue-collar workers; and (7) examines the impact of the "revolution in womanpower" for women themselves, their families, employers, and for education and other institutions.

Part Three of the Ginzberg work, "Manpower," deals with (1) federal manpower programs; (2) public service employment; (3) public and private policies to stimulate productivity; (4) the impact of a wide variety of federal policies — including immigration, health, and housing — on the development of, demand for, and utilization of human resources; (5) the need for research on urban manpower problems; (6) government as a "fourth factor" in production (in addition to land, labor, and capital); and (7) lessons from the Great Society.

The group which prepared the *OECD* volume concentrated on problems in the relationship between educational systems and working life, in light of social objectives of the OECD countries. Following a brief introduction, the OECD document recommends a "positive policy for working life," with suggestions addressed to governments, trade unions, and employers, and focused principally on the needs of "outsiders" — the disadvantaged, women, and migrant workers — to secure productive employment. Next, a series of recommendations is advanced in the name of an "integrative policy for education." Its major elements include (1) continuing (or recurrent) education for adults; (2) reducing disincentives for employment of youths; (3) financial aid for low-income upper-secondary students; (4) less "tracking" at the secondary level; (5) a blending of employment with full or part-time education; (6) reduction of constraints on admission to higher education; (7) greater options for youths, including expanded apprenticeships and a strengthening of noncollegiate forms of postsecondary education, such as employer-sponsored programs; (8) new opportunities for recurrent education, with preference accorded persons with low incomes or little previous schooling; and (9) improvement in basic instruction, so that young people are more equal at the starting line of adult life.

Next, the OECD group argues for greater options for the individual and reliance on the exercise of personal choice. The group advocates (1) development of alternative routes to credentials; (2) reliance on student choice in planning for education; (3) examination of ways to promote greater flexibility in patterns of life; (4) improved guidance from school to work and from work to retirement; and (5) the establishment at national, regional, and local levels of advisory machinery for dialogue on the contents of their report.

In effect, the OECD group argues that each individual should have five basic rights in the area of education and working life:

1. Basic education to age 16, with compensatory pedagogy and financing for those who need it;

2. Wider options — involving school, work, and service — for persons age 16 to 20;

3. Recurrent educational opportunities, with emphasis on those who earlier benefited least;

4. More emphasis on the quality of working life, including greater mobility and autonomy; and

5. Appropriate financing, and greater freedom to adjust the way each person uses his or her productive years for education, work, and leisure.

The *Wirtz* report — prepared on behalf of the National Manpower Institute and based on background material and a series of discussions involving two dozen leaders of industry, education, and the public — takes the view that to bring education and work closer together the need is not so much for new programs but for "truly *collaborative processes* among those in charge of these functions, including the 'public' " (Wirtz, 1975, p. v). Mankind is the "boundless resource" in the title of the report, a resource whose development is thought to depend more on coordination of work and education that on increasingly scarce natural resources.

The Wirtz report views positively both greater experiential learning for youths and greater opportunities for adults to return to school or college. Strategically, a case is presented for broadening activities on the basis of "established beachheads of consensus," with the involvement of educators, employer groups, and representatives of the public. The central recommendation is for a series of pilot efforts to test Community Education-Work Councils as the collaborative mechanisms for strengthening the links between education and work. Specific recommendations regarding youths are (1) identification of manpower needs and career prospects; (2) career guidance and counseling, including the placement of youths in jobs; (3) the meshing of liberal arts and vocational education; (4) expansion of work and service opportunities for young students; (5) making it possible for students to take a "considered break" from school; and (6) reducing barriers of law and tradition to youth employment. With respect to adults, the Wirtz report (1) calls for redesign of jobs to improve the quality of work life; (2) discusses the need for adult education, especially for those displaced by disability, trade, or technological developments; (3) recommends a national policy of up to four years worth of resources for further education of adults with less than a high school education; (4) advocates changes in unemployment insurance laws and retraining policy to foster countercyclical retraining; and (5) recommends tools such as external degree programs, flex-time, mobility incentives, and establishment of a national work institute to improve education, training, and work for adults. Particular attention is given to the needs of women, minorities, and older people — three groups which, in the judgment of Wirtz and his associates, may form the coalition necessary for a meaningful education-work policy.

Areas of Agreement

The four reports do not overlap on all areas but are

largely in agreement on the following topics:

- There is a need to reform and improve career guidance, counseling, and placement, especially for the non-college-bound and persons with poor family connections, by better selection and training of guidance personnel, provision of more useful information, greater employment of paraprofessionals and community resources, added attention to vocational and educational counseling, and the like.
- Persons who have once left the educational system should be encouraged to reenter at times in their lives when continuing or recurrent education will be of greatest value.
- It may be wise for some students to leave school temporarily for work or service, and education, work, and other institutions should be modified so as not to discourage "stopping out."
- Basic skills, liberal arts, vocational courses, and experiential learning all have a role in assisting young people to make career choices and to acquire and practice useful skills.
- There is room for change in legal constraints and customs regarding the employment of youths who have reached age 14 or 16.
- Employment and training programs since the early 1960s, while they promised more than they delivered, have had a beneficial impact on those served.
- Manpower and retraining programs should be strengthened and used more effectively to encourage training for persons without skills or with outmoded skills during recessionary phases of the business cycle.
- Youths, women, ethnic minorities, and older persons have a special stake in efforts to improve the links

between education and work and to facilitate greater individual choice as to the way in which each person uses his or her potentially productive years.

- Greater continuity in federal policy toward sciences and higher education would help reduce imbalances in the supply and demand for highly educated manpower.
- It would be helpful to have more accurate forecasts of supply and demand in markets for highly educated manpower and of the impact of changes in federal budget policy.
- Improvements in the relationships between education and employment are not the exclusive responsibility of educators.

Areas of Less Than Full Agreement

Our report is more agnostic than the Wirtz report as to the causes and solutions of youth unemployment. Wirtz and his colleagues attribute a good deal of the differential between youth and adult unemployment rates to structural difficulties. A common view in the Wirtz report is that, in the absence of specialized skills, young people must wait near the end of the unemployment line: "The situation is that with national unemployment at the 9 percent level, layoff lists are so long that the prospects of any young person's finding a job — college degree or not — has been sharply reduced except in a few relatively specialized fields."

The Wirtz report, unlike our report, often takes for granted the value of work and other experiences as part of a young person's educational program. Our report emphasizes qualitative differences in work-experience programs and differences in the readiness of individuals

225

to profit from such experience. The Wirtz volume asserts, for example, that "All the evidence suggests that education in the basic skills and humanities will be advanced, not retarded, by combining it with experience" (p. 55), and "Surveys made by the Department of Labor indicate that work experience results in (or is at least accompanied by) . . . significant improvements in school grades" (p. 60). As pointed out in our report, more than one study sponsored by the Department of Labor (e.g. Robin, 1969; Stromsdorfer, 1973a) point in the opposite direction.

Each of the four reports comments on the alleged oversupply of college graduates and concomitant individual frustration and social discontent. Because of recent improvements in the job outlook, our report is cautiously optimistic that the most serious imbalances have passed, and that the outlook for new college graduates in the years ahead is brighter than at any time in recent years.

Finally, our report is somewhat less pessimistic than Wirtz or Ginzberg as to the role that families play in assisting young people to acquire skills and to make career decisions. Ginzberg, while encouraging parents to visit schools, fears that the impact of parents may be negative as a result of community control of schools. Wirtz (pp. 41, 63) laments the fact that families to not perform their historical functions: "Today the role of the family seems almost negligible, although this is in some ways and to some extent an illusion" (p. 41). Our report suggests actions to strengthen the contribution of family life to the socialization of youths.

Research and Experimentation Needs

Of the four reports, the present one — because of its

mandate to review research and suggest fruitful lines of inquiry — devotes more attention to gaps in knowledge than the other three. The OECD document, the briefest of the lot, identifies the smallest number of research questions. The Ginzberg volume identifies a somewhat larger number. Among the three, the Wirtz book possesses the longest list.

All four of the reports recommend evaluation of the effectiveness of modern career guidance systems. Three (OECD, Wirtz, and NAE) urge experimentation with career guidance services offered outside the school in free-standing or community-based settings. Wirtz sees a need for better, more refined information on manpower demand and supply at the local level; Ginzberg and NAE express the need to inform governments, educational institutions and individuals as to developments in large and important markets for highly educated persons.

Wirtz, NAE, and OECD all identify important gaps in knowledge of the cost-benefit and equity implications of various patterns and sequences of work, service, and education. As Wirtz points out (p. 13): "There has been virtually no analysis of the maximally efficient, economic, and high-yield distribution of people's time as between work and education and recreation and leisure." Each report also notes the unknown costs or savings that might result from deliberately altering employer and educational priorities. As a specific suggestion, the OECD group recommends a study of educational drawing rights for youths 16 to 20 years of age. In a related vein, the Wirtz volume identifies a need for better statistics on paid and unpaid work, schooling, employment and its economic implications, and use of leisure time.

Ginzberg, Wirtz, and NAE identify important gaps in knowledge of the implications of various education, work, and service experiences for the subsequent well-being of individuals. Both the Wirtz report and NAE advocate longitudinal studies in this area. Ginzberg sees a need to evaluate various kinds of compensatory education for young people in school, the effectiveness of public service employment programs, and the influence of urban environments on families and individuals. Both NAE and Wirtz raise questions as to the value derived from various curricular options. The Wirtz report (p. 29), for example, asserts: "It is by no means clear that more sharply oriented education is less valuable than a general course of study, even if the particular opportunity prepared for turns out not to be available." Wirtz also calls attention to the absence of knowledge of the consequences of a variety of efforts since the early 1960s to tie education and work more closely together.

Other information gaps identified in the Wirtz volume include:

- The meaning and significance of high differential unemployment rates for youths and adults
- The comparative job performance of adults and youths with varying levels of education
- The relationships between work satisfaction and productivity
- The extent of unemployment among workers who, although securely attached to employers, have been displaced by technological or other developments and the cost of retraining such persons
- The effects of compulsory retirement on productivity and on the utilization of older persons

- The needs and interests of women after their children are raised
- Employer policies regarding the employment of youths and the assignment of persons under age 21 to youth-type jobs
- The nature, scope, and determinants of employer training and of employer training needs
- The laws, practices, and customs that influence the movement of people between education and work

Additional knowledge gaps raised by Ginzberg include:

- The acquisition of reading skills
- The relationships, if any, between working mothers and juvenile delinquency
- The "family as the unit of employment" and its effect on mobility
- The extensiveness of opportunities for blue-collar workers to improve their occupational position and to raise their income (here again, longitudinal research is advocated)
- The behavior of employers in urban areas in adjusting to a changing labor pool
- The decisions of firms to locate in urban areas or to move to suburbs
- The influence of intergovernmental relations on the urban environment
- A general need for social experimentation before initiation of major new social programs

Appendix C
Trends in Federal Expenditures
Related to Education and
Employment

Education in the United States is basically a state and local responsibility. Macroeconomic policies, including special efforts to offset the effects of unemployment through income transfers, jobs, and special training programs, are largely a federal responsibility. In Appendix C, we describe recent trends in federal outlays in areas where employment, education, and training overlap.[1]

Over the past ten years, federal budget outlays have been equal in magnitude to approximately one-fifth of the gross national product (see Table C.1). The proportion of the nation's output of goods and services actually purchased through the federal government is, of course, much smaller, since well over half of federal budget outlays represent income transfers from the taxpayer to individuals and families (as in the case of social security payments or interest on the public debt) or to state and local governments. Unfortunately, with the data that is available, we cannot separate transfer payments that go directly to individuals from those that go to state and local governments for distribution to individuals or for the purchase of goods and services.

Table C.1
Federal budget outlays by major category compared with the gross national product, fiscal years 1968 to 1977

		Federal budget outlays as percent of GNP		
	GNP[a]		Goods	Transfer
Fiscal	(millions		and	payments
year	of $)	Total	services	and other[b]
1977	$1,890	21.3%	7.3%	14.0%
1976	1,692	22.1	7.9	14.2
1975	1,516	21.7	7.8	13.9
1974	1,413	19.7	7.4	12.3
1973	1,307	19.6	7.8	11.8
1972	1,171	19.9	8.6	11.3
1971	1,063	20.0	8.9	11.1
1970	982	19.9	9.9	9.9
1969	930	19.9	10.5	9.3
1968	864	20.7	11.0	9.7

[a] GNP is for calendar rather than fiscal year.

[b] Includes transfer payments, grants-in-aid to state and local governments, and net interest paid.

Sources: U.S. Department of Commerce, *Survey of Current Businesses* (1978) and Office of Management and Budget (1978), p. 21.

Federal budget outlays vary in a countercyclical fashion. In the recession year of 1971 and again during the most recent downturn in economic activity (from 1974 to 1976), federal outlays — especially in the form of transfer payments — increased in relation to GNP. Indeed, the spectacular rise in transfer payments since 1970 is perhaps the major development in the use of federal funds since 1970. In the year ending June 30, 1970, just under $100 billion in federal money was spent for goods and services, and an almost identical amount was distributed in transfers to individuals and to other levels of government. By the end of fiscal year 1975, federal outlays for goods and services had increased to only $118 billion while transfers had shot up to $211 billion. A portion of the latter increase is attributable to a very substantial rise in unemployment compensation and similar income maintenance expenditures.

Over the past few years, federal expenditures for education, training, employment, and social services have risen slightly faster than total federal outlays (Table C.2). The amount spent for such purposes, at about $20 billion per year, represents approximately 5 percent of the total federal budget.

Table C.2
Percentage of federal budget outlays, by function, fiscal years 1974 to 1979

Budget function	1974	1975	1976	1977	1978	1979
Total (billions of $)	$268.4	$324.6	$366.5	$411.2	$440.0	$500.2
National defense	29.3%	26.7%	24.6%	24.3%	25.5%	23.6%
International affairs	1.3	1.3	1.4	1.7	1.7	1.5
General science, space, and technology	1.5	1.2	1.2	1.1	1.1	1.0
Natural resources, environment, and energy	2.4	2.9	3.1	4.1	4.5	4.4
Agriculture	.8	.5	.7	.7	.5	1.1
Commerce and transportation	4.9	4.9	4.7	3.9	4.4	4.1
Community and regional development	1.8	1.4	1.4	1.9	1.8	1.7
Education, training, employment, and social services	4.3	4.7	5.0	5.1	4.4	6.1
Health	8.2	8.5	9.1	9.5	9.8	9.9
Income security	31.5	33.5	34.8	33.6	32.7	32.0
Veterans benefits and services	5.0	5.1	5.0	4.5	4.2	3.9
Law enforcement and justice	.9	.9	.9	.9	.9	.8
General government	1.2	1.0	.8	.9	.9	.9

Revenue sharing and general purpose fiscal assistance	2.5	2.2	1.9	2.2	1.8	1.9
Interest	10.5	9.5	9.4	9.2	9.0	9.8
Undistributed offsetting receipts	-6.2	-4.3	-4.0	-3.7	-3.7	-3.2

Source: U.S. Office of Management and Budget, 1977a, pp. 426-431; 1978, pp. 76-81.

234

The federal budget categories, however, are far from ideal in assessing the way in which federal funds are spent. Simply to illustrate, in the case of education, a rather sizeable portion of expenditures for veterans enables members of this group to attend college or participate in other forms of postsecondary education and training. Yet, such expenditures, instead of being budgeted with education and training funds, are part of "veterans benefits and services," along with other veterans allocations that have nothing to do with education. Table C.3, which draws upon the classification scheme developed by the National Center for Education Statistics, reveals that only about one-third of federal outlays for education are administered by the Department of Health, Education, and Welfare. The Departments of Agriculture, Defense, and Labor, together with the Veterans Administration, administer sizable educational programs. By levels of the educational system, over one-third of the total goes to provide support for college students, for instruction, research, or service provided by institutions of higher learning.

Table C.3
Federal funds for education by level of education and by source, fiscal year 1977

	Millions of Dollars	Percent
Total	$23,328.7	100.0%
Level:		
Elementary-secondary	$ 4,714.4	20.2%
Higher education	8,508.9	36.5
Vocational, technical, and continuing	3,837.5	16.4
Other education	6,268.0	26.9
Source:		
DHEW	8,164.9	35.0
Education Division	(6,452.8)	(27.7)
Other HEW	(1,712.1)	(7.3)
Department of Agriculture	2,243.6	9.6
Department of Defense	1,406.9	6.0
Department of Labor	2,795.0	12.0
Veterans Administration	4,153.4	17.8
All other agencies	1,110.9[a]	4.8
Research and development in colleges and universities (all agencies)	3,454.0[b]	14.8

[a] Includes NCES estimate of $144.5 million appropriated for use by the District of Columbia.

[b] Estimate for fiscal year 1977.

Source: U.S. Office of Management and Budget (1977a, 1977b); U.S. National Center for Education Statistics (1977), pp. 164-166; and National Science Foundation (1976).

Mangum (1976) has classified expenditures in a somewhat different and overlapping way to analyze the use of federal funds for employment and training (Table C.4). In response to economic conditions — and doubtless reflecting as well the skepticism which emerged in the early 1970s over the effectiveness of manpower training — skill training, especially of the institutional or classroom type, has decreased in relative importance since 1965, while public service employment and work experience programs for out-of-school youths and adults have increased sharply in both relative and absolute terms.

Table C.4
Percentage of federal outlays for various types of employment and training programs, fiscal years 1965, 1970, and 1975

	1965	1970	1975
Total (millions of $)	$798	$2,546	$6,177
Skill training, total	47.7%	54.5%	36.0%
Institutional training	29.7	24.1	12.6
On-the-job training	4.3	11.0	7.7
Vocational rehabilitation	13.8	19.4	15.6
Work support, total	17.4%	19.0%	40.0%
In-school	12.5	10.3	8.0
Post-school	4.9	8.6	12.4
Public service employment	—	—	19.6
Labor market services, total	30.8%	20.9%	21.3%
Job placement	25.6	14.6	9.4
Anti-discrimination	—	0.7	1.5
Employment-related child care	5.3	5.5	8.0
Other (various)	—	—	2.4
Administration, research and support	4.0%	5.6%	2.7%

Source: Mangum (1976), pp. 57-62.

Federal outlays in fiscal year 1977, for education and related activities, by agency and level of education, are presented in Table C.5. Where expenditures range across levels or types of institutions, program outlays have been allocated to each level. To illustrate, $393 million in federal funds was spent for occupational, vocational, and adult education in elementary and secondary schools. An additional $166 million went principally to two-year institutions of higher education.

Finally, an additional $129 million was spent for adult basic and vocational education in a variety of settings, including public libraries, but also involving skills centers, community colleges, and adult high schools.

Table C.5
Federal outlays for education and
related activities, fiscal year 1977

	Millions of dollars

Elementary and secondary:

Early childhood:

Office of Education:

Elementary and secondary............................371

Education for the handicapped 52

Appalachian regional development.....................14

Human development services 458

Other 20

         Subtotal, early childhood.....................915

Elementary and secondary:

Child nutrition..................................2,792

Defense...271

Office of Education:

Educationally deprived children 1,716

Other elementary and secondary programs 267

Federally affected areas 765

Emergency school aid 22

Education for the handicapped 111

Occupational, vocational, and adult education 393

Library resources and library consolidation............112

Other, Office of Education 47

Student grants, Social Security Administration...........314

Other HEW.......................................120

Bureau of Indian Affairs, Interior 193

U.S. Forest Service, Agriculture 25

Veterans readjustment 92

Other 69

         Subtotal, elementary and secondary 7,309

Millions
of dollars

Supporting services:
  Office of Education:
    Educationally deprived children 64
    Other elementary and secondary programs 82
    Support and innovation 48
    Education for the handicapped 83
    Special projects and training 20
  National Institute of Education 43
  National Science Foundation 3
  Other 15

    Subtotal 358

    Total 8,582

Higher education:

2-year institutions:
  Office of Education:
    Basic opportunity grants 694
    Other higher education 291
    Occupational and vocational education. 166
  Student grants, Social Security Administration 282
  Health Resources Administration 45
  Veterans readjustment 1,451
  Other 87

    Subtotal, 2-year institutions 3,016

Other undergraduate:
  Military service academies 245
  Reserve Officers Training Corps 183
  Health Resources Administration 73
  Office of Education:
    Basic opportunity grants 694
    Work-study and supplementary grants 403
    Guaranteed student loans 204
    Direct student loans. 181
    Disadvantaged students and developing institutions 103
    Other higher education 242
  Student grants, Social Security Administration 863

240

	Millions of dollars
Special institutions	46
Office of the Secretary	68
Other Office of Education and HEW	24
Bureau of Indian Affairs, Interior	27
Veterans readjustment	1,062
National Science Foundation	24
Other	64
Subtotal, other undergraduate	4,506

Graduate and professional:

Health Services Administration	27
Research training, National Institutes of Health	125
Alcohol, Drug, and Mental Health Administration	63
Health Resources Administration	539
Higher education (Office of Education)	71
Student grants, Social Security Administration	36
Special institutions	53
Veterans readjustment	289
Department of Defense	208
National Science Foundation	25
Other	82
Subtotal, graduate and professional	1,518
Total	9,040

Adult education and other activities:

Adult basic and extension:

Agriculture extension service	239
Occupational, vocational and adult education	129
Other Office of Education	77
Social Security Administration	118
Veterans readjustment	512
Department of Defense	87
Other	27
Subtotal, adult basic and extension	1,189

Public and national library services:

Library of Congress	88
Library resources (Office of Education)	42
Other	26
Subtotal, public and national library services	156

	Millions of dollars

Training of Federal, State, and local civilian employees:

Justice	13
Federal Aviation Administration	17
Commerce Department	11
Department of the Treasury	11
Other	11
Subtotal, training of public civilian employees	63

Training of Federal military employees:

Defense	339
Coast Guard	25
Subtotal, training of Federal military employees	364

Foreign educational activities:

International development assistance	60
Department of Defense	2
Subtotal, foreign educational activities	62

Other:

Office of Education:

Salaries and expenses	118
Educationally deprived children	56
Assistant Secretary for Education	22
Special institutions	33
Office of the Secretary, HEW	34
National Institutes of Health	21
Smithsonian Institution	58
Corporation for Public Broadcasting	103
National Endowments for the Arts and Humanities	16
Public service jobs, Labor	462
Housing and Urban Development	-44
International Communication Agency	34
Other	69
Subtotal, other	982
Total	2,816
GRAND TOTAL	20,438

Source: Office of Management and Budget (1978), pp. 224-227.

While there may be some slight overlap, federal outlays for training and employment programs are shown in Table C.6. In 1977, about $9.1 billion were spent for such purposes, comparable with $20.4 billion for education and other basic purposes involving educational institutions.

Table C.6
Federal outlays for training and
employment programs, fiscal year 1977

	Millions of dollars
Department of Health Education and Welfare:	
Social services manpower	667
High school work-study	10
Vocational rehabilitation	897
CETA support	2
National occupational information coordinating committee	—
Subtotal, HEW	1,575
Department of Labor:	
Employment and training assistance	3,291
Temporary employment assistance	2,340
Work incentive program (WIN)	361
Employment Service	604
Older American community service employment	72
Food stamp recipient services	29
Labor market information	28
Equal employment opportunity	7
Program administration	98
Employment opportunities program	—
Subtotal, Labor	6,829
Department of Agriculture: Youth Conservation Corps	48
Department of Commerce: Job opportunities program	98
Department of the Interior: Indian programs	49
Department of Justice: Prisoner training	1
Department of Housing and Urban Development:	
Community development	12

	Millions of dollars
Veterans Administration:	
On-the-job training	175
Vocational rehabilitation	109
Assistance centers	9
Community Services Administration:	
Senior opportunities and services	1
Equal Employment Opportunity Commission:	
Equal employment opportunity enforcement	72
Other Federal agencies:	
Federal contract compliance	7
Summer youth programs	140
Subtotal, Other agencies	721
TOTAL	9,125

Source: Office of Management and Budget (1978), p. 241.

---

[1]/Budget figures, however, tell only a part of the story of federal policies and their impact on manpower supply, demand, and utilization. Ginzberg (1975, Chapter 19) reminds us that policies in many areas — immigration, social security, health, defense, space, research and development, agricultural supports, housing, transportation, labor laws, and taxes — play a role well beyond annual budgetary outlays.

Members of the Task Force

David W. Breneman
Senior Fellow
The Brookings Institution

Mr. Breneman taught economics at Amherst College from 1970 to 1972. He served as Staff Director of the National Board of Graduate Education, National Academy of Sciences (NAS), from 1972 to 1975 and while on leave from Brookings as Deputy Assistant Secretary of Education, Policy Development/ Designate, in 1977. Mr. Breneman is a member of the US/USSR Exchange Seminar on Manpower Forecasting, the Governing Board of National Enquiry into Scholarly Communication, the National Science Foundation Advisory Panel on University and Non-Profit Institutions Study Group, and the NAS Committee on Environmental Manpower.

Mr. Breneman has written and talked extensively on graduate education and federal policy toward higher education. His writings include *Forecasting the Ph.D. Labor Market* (with Freeman), *Graduate School Adjustments to the "New Depression" in Higher Education*, and *Public Policy and Private Higher Education* (co-editor with Finn).

Richard B. Freeman
Professor of Economics
Harvard University

Mr. Freeman taught at Yale University and the University of Chicago before returning to Harvard in the early 1970s. He has been a consultant to a number of organizations, including the National Science Foundation Task Force on Academic Salaries, the Congressional Budget Office and Office of Technology Assessment, the National Board of Graduate Education, and the Organization for Economic Cooperation and Development (OECD). He served as Research Economist for the Area Redevelopment Administration in 1964, for the Committee for Economic Development in 1965, and for the Harvard Economic Research Project from 1967 to 1971. He is Director of Research at the National Bureau of Economic Research.

Mr. Freeman has written numerous articles and books on markets for skills and high-level manpower, social mobility, discrimination, income distribution, trade unionism, and economic history and development. Among his works are *The Overeducated American, Black Elite, Labor Market Analysis of Engineers and Technical Workers* (with Cain and Hansen), *Labor Economics*, and *Forecasting the Ph.D. Labor Market* (with Breneman).

William Gomberg
Professor of Management and Industrial Relations
The Wharton School, University of Pennsylvania

Mr. Gomberg worked for the International Ladies Garment Workers' Union in New York City, first as a collective bargaining representative (1934-1941) and later as Director of the union's Management Engineering

Department (1941-1956), where he pioneered the concept of industrial engineering as a tool in collective bargaining. Before his appointment to the staff of the Wharton School, he taught at Washington University in St. Louis, the University of California, and Columbia University.

Mr. Gomberg has taught in special courses and programs at several universities, including Stanford, Columbia, and Wisconsin. He has been a consultant to many organizations, including the Department of Commerce, the National Academy of Sciences, the American Federation of Labor, the United Automobile Workers, the International Association of Machinists, United Textile Workers, Continental Air Lines, Inc., the Ronson Corporation, American Standard, Inc., and Merck, Sharp and Dohme. Since 1949, he has served as an arbitrator in several industries, including steel, automobile, electrical goods, textile clothing, and transportation. He recently monitored for the Atlantic Richfield Corporation a project to prepare minority group members for business opportunities in service stations. He directed a University of Pennsylvania program to train minority group members for positions in educational administration. He is a member of the Board of Directors of the Aspen Institute for Humanistic Studies.

Mr. Gomberg is a frequent speaker in executive development programs and has written several books and articles, including *Blue Collar World* (with Shostak), *New Perspectives on Poverty* (with Shostak), *Lessons from the Hardcore Unemployed: Some Implications for Entrepreneurial Thinking — Study of an Atlantic Richfield Corporate Experiment*, and *Due Process Theory of Management* (in progress).

Clark Kerr, Chairman of the Task Force
Chairperson
Carnegie Council on Policy Studies in Higher Education

Mr. Kerr served as President of the University of California from 1958 to 1967 and as Chairman of the Carnegie Commission on Higher Education from 1967 to 1973. Mr. Kerr was a member of President Eisenhower's Commission on National Goals (1959-1960), is a member of the board of several nonprofit institutions, including Swarthmore College and the Work in America Institute, and chaired the Secretary-General's Ad Hoc Group on the Relations Between Education and Employment of the Organization for Economic Cooperation and Development (1973-1974).

Mr. Kerr has authored numerous articles and books, including *Unions, Management and the Public* (with Bakke), *Industrialism and Industrial Man* (with Dunlop, Harbison, and Myers), *The Uses of the University, Labor and Management in Industrial Society, Industrialism and Industrial Man Reconsidered* (with Dunlop, Harbison, and Myers), *Labor Markets and Wage Determination,* and *Education and Working Life in Modern Society,* a report for the OECD (with others).

Ewald B. Nyquist
Vice-President for Academic Development
Pace University

Mr. Nyquist served as Assistant Director and Director of University Admissions at Columbia University before joining the New York Education Department in 1951. There, he held a succession of positions, from Assistant Commissioner for Higher Education (1951-1955) to Commissioner of Education and President of The University of The State of New York (1969-1977).

In his inaugural address in 1970, he proposed the Regents External Degree Program, which came to fruition shortly thereafter.

Mr. Nyquist has been active in the field of accreditation. He was chairman from 1953 to 1959 of the Commission on Institutions of Higher Education of the Middle States Association of Colleges and Secondary Schools. He is a member of several visiting committees, councils, and boards, including the Rand Corporation Advisory Board on Education and Human Resources and the Commission on Collegiate Athletics (Chairman), sponsored by the American Council on Education. He has received many awards, including more than 25 honorary doctoral degrees.

Mr. Nyquist is the author of numerous articles, speeches, and books, including: *Open Education, a Sourcebook for Parents and Teachers* (with Hawes), *College Learning Any time, Anywhere* (with others), "The Role of the State in Urban Education," the Harlan E. Anderson Lecture, Yale University (1971), "Issues of Reform in Higher Education," the First Novice Fawcett Lecture, The Ohio State University (1972), and "Work, Business and Education (with Comments on Immorality and Inefficiency)," The First Peter L. Agnew Memorial Lecture, New York University (1976).

John R. Shea, Staff Assistant to the Task Force
Senior Fellow
Carnegie Council on Policy Studies in Higher Education

Mr. Shea taught at the University of Santa Clara from 1965 to 1966; served as chief of The Ohio State University's human resources planning team in Bolivia from 1966 to 1968; taught at The Ohio State University and was Associate Director of the National Longitudinal

Surveys Project from 1968 to 1972; served as Senior Research Associate on the Carnegie Commission staff in 1973; and from 1973 to 1975 was an Associate Research Economist in the Center for Research and Development in Higher Education, University of California, Berkeley.

Mr. Shea has authored several articles and books, including a chapter in *Youth Unemployment and Minimum Wages*, BLS Bulletin 1657: *Dual Careers, Career Thresholds, and Years for Decision*, Manpower Research Monographs 16, 21, and 24 (with others); a chapter in *The Impact of Manpower Programs: An Evaluation* (Michael Borus, ed.); staff material for the Carnegie Commission's *Toward a Learning Society; Presidents Confront Reality* (with Glenny, Ruyle, and Freschi); and *Extending Opportunities for the College Degree* (with Medsker, Edelstein, Ruyle, and Kreplin).

Patricia Snider
Demographer
Human Resources Management Activity,
   General Motors Corporation

Ms. Snider served as Research Sociologist at Battelle's Columbus Laboratories from 1973 to 1975. She is a member of several organizations, including the Statistical Committee of the Equal Employment Advisory Council, American Women in Science, and Women's Equity Action League.

Ms. Snider is author of *Human Resources Planning: A Guide to Data* (with Royer and Baytos), a publication of the Equal Employment Advisory Council, and "External Data for Affirmative Action Planning," a paper presented at a Cornell Conference on Affirmative Action Planning Concepts in 1977.

E. Belvin Williams
Senior Vice President
Educational Testing Service

Mr. Williams held a series of positions at Teachers College, Columbia University, from 1961 to 1972, before joining the ETS as Vice President for Operations. He was Director of the Teacher's College Computer Center from 1964 to 1971 and Associate Professor of Psychology and Education as well as Associate Dean from 1970 to 1972. Mr. Williams has served as a consultant to a number of organizations: Belmar Computer Services, Inc., the Peace Corps and Teachers Corps, the SEEK Program at Hunters College of the City University of New York, Metropolitan Mental Health Clinic, the Fresh Air Fund, and National Urban League. He recently chaired an ETS Review Committe on the Testing of Minorities and was Chairman for the Northeast Region of the Association of Black Psychologists in 1969.

Mr. Williams is a member of the Harvard Board of Overseers; served on the New York State Committee for Children from 1971 to 1974; is a Trustee of the Dalton Schools, New York City; and is on the Board of Directors of A Better Chance, Inc.

Mr. Williams' writings include work on schizophrenia, contributions to *Introduction to Psychology* (by F. Ruch), "The Association Between Smoking and Accidents" in *Traffic Quarterly* (1966), and *Driving and Connotative Meanings* (with Malfetti).

Bibliography

ACTION. *Americans Volunteer — 1974*. Washington, D.C.: U.S. Government Printing office, 1975.

Adams, F.C. and Stephens, C.W. *College and University Student Work Programs: Implications and Implementations*. Carbondale, Ill.: Southern Illinois University Press, 1970.

Advisory Panel on the Scholastic Aptitude Test Score Decline, W. Wirtz, Chairman, *On Further Education*, Report of the Panel. New York: College Entrance Examination Board, 1977.

Allen, B.V. "Paying Students to Learn," *Personnel and Guidance Journal* Vol. 53, No. 10, June 1975, pp. 774-777.

Andrisani, P.J. *An Empirical Analysis of the Dual Labor Market Theory*. Columbus, Ohio: The Ohio State University, Center for Human Resources, 1973.

Arbeiter, S. *Career Transitions: The Demand for Counseling*, Volume 1. New York: Policy Studies in Education, a Department of Educational Research Council of America, 1976.

Arrow, K. "Higher Education as a Filter." *Journal of Public Economics*. Vol. 2, No. 3, July 1973, pp. 193-216.

Arthur D. Little, Inc. *Documented Employer Benefits from Co-operative Education*. Summary of a Report of a Study for Northeastern University. Boston: Author, May 1974.

Ashenfelter, O., and others. *Evaluating Manpower Training Programs*. Papers presented at a conference sponsored by the Industrial Relations Section, Princeton University, and the Office of the Assistant Secretary of Labor for Policy, Evaluation, and Research. (Unpublished, 1976).

Astin, A.W., and others. *The American Freshman: National Norms for Fall 1973*, Los Angeles: Cooperative Institutional

Research Program, University of California, Los Angeles, 1974.

Augsburger, J.D. "An Analysis of Academic Performance of Working and Non-working Students on Academic Probation at Northern Illinois University." *Journal of Student Financial Aid*, 4(2), June 1974, pp. 30-38.

Bachman, J.G. *Youth in Transition, Vol. III, Dropping Out — Problem or Symptom?* Ann Arbor, Michigan: Institute for Social Research, 1971.

Baker, H.B. "The Working Student and His Grades." *Journal of Educational Research*, Vol. 35, 1941, pp. 28-35.

Barton, P. "Juvenile Delinquency, Work, and Education." Paper prepared by the National Manpower Institute for the Education Division, Department of Health, Education, and Welfare (unpublished), August 1976.

Becker, G.S. *Human Capital*, New York: Columbia University Press for the National Bureau of Economic Research, 1964.

Becker, G.S. "A Theory of the Allocation of Time," *Economic Journal*, Vol. LXXV (September, 1965), pp. 493-517.

Benham, L. "The Effect of Advertising on the Price of Eyeglasses." *Journal of Law and Economics*, Vol. 15: 1972, pp. 337-352.

Berg, I. *Education and Jobs: The Great Training Robbery.* Boston: Beacon Press, 1970.

Best, F. and Stern, B. "Lifetime Distribution of Education, Work, and Leisure: Research, Speculations, and Policy Implications of Changing Life Patterns." Paper presented at the Monthly Dialogue on Lifelong Learning (November 8, 1976), sponsored by the Postsecondary Education Convening Authority, Institute for Educational Leadership, The George Washington University, December 1976.

Bird, C. *The Case Against College.* New York: David McKay Co., Inc., 1975.

Bisconti, A.S., and Solman, L.C. *College Education on the Job — The Graduates Viewpoint.* Bethleham, Pa.: The CPC Foundation, 1976.

Borus, M.E., Brennan, J.P., and Rosen, S. "A Benefit-Cost Analysis of the Neighborhood Youth Corps." *Journal of Human Resources*, Vol. (2), Spring 1970, pp. 139-159.

Bowen, Howard R. *Investment in Learning: The Individual and*

253

Social Value of American Higher Education. San Francisco: Jossey-Bass Publishers, 1977.

Bowles, E. "Older Persons as Providers of Services: Three Federal Programs." *Social Policy,* November-December 1976, pp. 81-88.

Bowlsbey, J.A.N. "Sex Bias and Computer-Based Guidance Systems," in E.E. Diamond (ed.) *Issues of Sex Bias and Sex Fairness in Career Interest Measurement.* Washington, D.C.: NIE, 1975.

Budd, W.C. "The Effect of Outside Employment on Initial Academic Adjustment in College." *College and University,* 31(2). 1956, pp. 220-223.

Burkhardt, C., Orletsky, S.R., Hotchkiss, H.L., Lowry, C.M., Curry, E.W., and Campbell, R.E. *Involving Significant Others in Career Planning: A Counselor's Handbook.* Research and Development Survey No. 128. Columbus, Ohio: Center for Vocational Education, The Ohio State University, July, 1977.

Cain, G.G. "The Challenge of Segmented Labor Market Theories to Orthodox Theory: A Survey." *Journal of Economic Literature.* Vol. 14, No. 4, December 1976, pp. 1215-1257.

Cairnes, J.E. *Some Leading Principles of Political Economy Newly Expounded.* New York, Harper and Grothers, 1874.

California Postsecondary Education Commission, *Veterinary Medical Education in California: An Assessment of the Need for Expansion.* Report 76-5 (April 1976).

Campbell, A., Converse, P.E., and Rodgers, W.L. *The Quality of American Life: Perceptions, Evaluations, and Satisfactions.* New York: Russell Sage Foundation, 1976.

Campbell, David. *The Results of Counseling: Twenty-Five Years Later.* (1965).

Campbell, R.E. *Vocational Guidance in Secondary Education: Results of a Survey.* Columbus, Ohio: Center for Vocational and Technical Education, The Ohio State University, 1968.

Carey, M.L. "Revised Occupational Projections to 1985." *Monthly Labor Review,* 99, (11) November 1976, pp. 10-22.

Carlson, R.J. "Health, Manpower Licensing and Emerging Institutional Responsibility for the Quality of Care." *Law and Contemporary Problems.* Vol. 35, Autumn 1970, pp. 849-878.

Cartter, A. "The Supply of and Demand for College Teachers."

The *Journal of Human Resources*, Vol. 1, No. 1, Winter 1965, pp. 23-28.

Center for Human Resource Research, The Ohio State University. *The National Longitudinal Surveys Handbook.* Columbus Ohio: 1977.

Chrysler, E. "Estimating the Supply and Demand for Animal Health Care." A Research Report Presented to the California Veterinary Medical Association. (Duplicated; March 1976).

Cicourel, A.V. and Kitsuse, J.I. *The Educational Decision-Makers.* Indianapolis, Indiana: Bob-Merrill, 1963.

Cole, N.S., and Hanson, G.R. "Impact of Interest Inventories and Career Choice," in E.E. Diamond (ed.). *Issues of Sex Bias and Sex Fairness in Career Interest Measurement.* Washington, D.C.: NIE, 1975.

Coleman, J.S., et al. *Equality of Educational Opportunity.* Washington, D.C.: GPO, 1966.

Committee on Education and Labor, U.S. House of Representatives. *Hearings Before the Special Subcommittee on Education and Student Financial Assistance* (Work Programs) May 7, 8, 13, 14, 15, 16, and 21, 1974. Washington, D.C.: GPO, 1974.

Cooley, T.F., McGuire, T.W., and Prescott, E.C. *The Impact of Manpower Training on Earnings: An Econometric Analysis.* Report MEL 76-01. Contract No. 43-4-001-42, for the Office of Program Evaluation, ETA/DOL. Washington, D.C.: GPO, 1976.

Council of State Governments. *The States and Medical Malpractice.* A Research Brief. Lexington, Ky.: July 1975.

Creager, J.A., and others. *National Norms for Entering College Freshmen — Fall 1968.* Washington, D.C.: American Council on Education, 1968.

Cremin, L.A. *Public Education.* New York: Basic Book, Inc., Publishers, 1976.

Crites, J.O. *Vocational Psychology: The Study of Vocational Behavior and Development.* New York: McGraw-Hill Book Co., 1969.

Cross, K.P. *The Integration of Learning and Earning: Cooperative Education and Nontraditional Study.* ERIC/Higher Education Research Report No. 4. Washington, D.C.: American Association for Higher Education, 1973.

Denison, E.F. "Measuring the Contribution of Education (and the Residual) to Economic Growth." *The Residual Factor and Economic Growth.* OECD Study Group in the Economics of Education, 1964, pp. 13-15.

Diamond, E.E. (ed.) *Issues of Sex Bias and Sex Fairness in Career Interest Measurement.* Washington, D.C.: NIE, Spring 1975.

Doeringer, P.B. and Piore, M.J. *Internal Labor Markets and Manpower Analysis.* Lexington, Mass.: D.C. Heath and Co., 1971.

Drewes, D.W. and Katz, D.S. *Manpower Data and Vocational Education: A National Study of Availability and Use.* Raleigh, N.C.: Center for Occupational Education, North Carolina State University, 1975.

Dunlop, J.T. "The Task of Contemporary Wage Theory." *New Concepts in Wage Discrimination.* Edited by George W. Taylor and Frank C. Pierson. New York: McGraw-Hill, 1957, pp. 117-39.

Dunn, P. and Dunn, K. *How to Raise Independent and Professionally Successful Daughters.* 1977.

Eckaus, R. "Returns to Education with Standardized Incomes." *Quarterly Journal of Economics.* Vol. 87, February 1973, pp. 121-131.

Ehrenberg, R.G. and Hewlett, J.G. "The Impact of the WIN 2 Program on Welfare Costs and Recipient Rates," *Journal of Human Resources.* Vol. XI, No. 2., (Spring 1976), pp. 219-232.

Elliott, D. and Knowles, B. *An Evaluation of the Oakland Youth Work Experience Program,* A Progress Report to the National Office for Social Responsibility. Boulder, Colorado: Behavioral Research Institute, June 1976.

Enderlein, T.E. "A Review of Career Education Studies." (Unpublished paper; Office of Career Education, USOE, n.d.).

Endicott, Frank S. *Trends in Employment of College and University Graduates in Business and Industry.* The Endicott Report. Evanson, Ill.: Northwestern University, 1975.

Farber, D. *An Analysis of Change in Earnings of Participants in Manpower Training Programs.* Internal, unpublished report. Washington, D.C.: U.S. Department of Labor, 1972.

Faulk, D.C. "Job Expectations and Unemployment Among Young Women with Work Experience." (M.A. thesis, The Ohio State University, 1972).

Federal Security Agency War Manpower Commission. *Federal Report of the National Youth Administration, Fiscal Years 1936-1943.* Washington, D.C.: GPO, 1944, pp. 75-77.

Feldstein, M. "The Economics of the New Unemployment." *Public Interest,* No. 33, Fall 1973, pp. 3-42.

Fine, B. *Underachievers: How They Can Be Helped.* New York: Dutton, 1966.

Fine, R.E. and others. *Final Report, AFDC Employment and Referral Guidelines.* Minneapolis, Minn.: Institute for Interdisciplinary Studies, June 1972.

Fowler, C. *New York Times,* May 4, 1977.

Freedman, M. *Labor Markets: Segments and Shelters.* Montclair, N.J.: Allanheld, Osmun & Co., 1976.

Freeman, R.B. "The Decline in the Economic Rewards to College Education." *Review of Economics and Statistics,* Vol. LIX, No. 1, pp. 18-29.

Freeman, R.B. *The Market for College Trained Manpower: A Study in the Economics of Career Choice.* Cambridge, Mass.: Harvard University Press, 1971.

Freeman, R.B., and Breneman, D. *Forecasting the Ph.D. Labor Market: Pitfalls for Policy.* Technical Report No. 2. Washington, D.C.: National Board on Graduate Education, 1974.

Freeman, R.B. *The Overeducated American.* New York: Academic Press, 1976.

Friedman, N., Sanders, L.W., and Thompson, J. *The Federal College Work-Study Program.* New York: Columbia University, Bureau of Applied Social Research, 1973.

Froomkin, J., and Wolfson, R.J. *Adult Education 1972, A Reanalysis.* Washington, D.C.: Joseph Froomkin Inc., May 1977.

Fuchs, V.R. *Who Shall Live? Health, Economics, and Social Choice.* New York, Basic Books, Inc., 1974.

Fullerton, H.N., Jr. and Flaim, P.D. "New Labor Force Projections to 1990." *Monthly Labor Review,* Vol. 99, No. 12, December 1976, pp. 3-13.

Ginzberg, E. *Career Guidance: Who Needs It, Who Provides It, Who Can Improve It.* New York: McGraw-Hill, 1971.

Ginzberg, E. *Life Styles of Educated Women.* New York: McGraw-Hill, 1966.

257

Ginzberg, E. *The Manpower Connection: Education and Work.* Cambridge, Mass.: Harvard University Press, 1975.

Ginzberg, E., et al. *Occupational Choice: An Approach to a General Theory.* New York: Columbia University Press, 1951.

Glover, R.W. and Marshall, R. *Training and Entry into Union Construction.* Manpower Research and Development Monograph 39. Washington, D.C.: GPO, 1975.

Goldstein, J.H. *The Effectiveness of Manpower Training Programs: A Review of Research on the Impact of the Poor.* U.S. Congress, Joint Economic Committee, 1972.

Gordon, D.M. *Theories of Poverty and Underemployment.* Lexington, Mass.: Heath, Lexington Books, 1972.

Gordon, M.S. "U.S. Manpower and Employment Policy," *Monthly Labor Review,* 87, Part 2, November 1964, pp. 1314-1321.

Gordon, M.S. *Retraining and Labor Market Adjustment in Western Europe.* Berkeley, Calif.: Institute of Industrial Relations, University of California, 1965.

Gordon, M. (ed.) *Higher Education and The Labor Market.* New York: McGraw-Hill, 1974.

Gordon, M.S. *Under-Education or Over-Education? The Outcomes of American Higher Education,* preliminary draft (unpublished manuscript, June 1977).

Gordon, R.A. "Another Look at the Goals of Full Employment and Price Stability." *Demographic Trends and Full Employment,* a report of the National Commission for Manpower Policy, Special Report No. 12 (December 1976). Reprint No. 418, Institute of Industrial Relations, UCB, 1977, pp. 1-26.

Gore, G. "New Evidence of Co-op System Relevancy." *The Journal of Cooperative Education,* Vol, 8, May 1972, pp. 7-14.

Gramlich, E.M. "Impact of Minimum Wages on Other Wages, Employment, and Family Incomes." *Brookings Papers on Economic Activity,* Vol. 2, 1976, pp. 409-451.

Grandy, T.G. *The Influence of the Family Upon the Expressed Occupational Choices of College Freshmen.* Unpublished M.A. Thesis, College of Education, University of Iowa, 1973.

Grasso, J.T. "On the Declining Labor Market Value of Schooling," paper presented at 1977 Annual Meeting of the American Educational Research Association (unpublished), 1977.

258

Grasso, J.T. *The Contributions of Vocational Education, Training, and Work Experience to the Early Career Achievements of Young Men.* Special Report. Columbus, Ohio: Center for Human Resource Research, The Ohio State University, July, 1975.

Grasso, J.T. and Shea, J.R. *Vocational Education and Training: Impact on Youth.* Berkeley, California: Carnegie Council on Policy Studies in Higher Education, 1979.

Griliches, Z. "Schooling Interruption, Work While in School, and the Returns from Schooling." Discussion Paper No. 529, Cambridge, Mass.: Harvard Institute of Economic Research, January 1977.

Hanoch, G. "An Economic Analysis of Earnings and Schooling." *Journal of Human Resources,* 2(3), Summer 1967, pp. 310-329.

Hansen, W.L. "Total and Private Rates of Return to Investment in Schooling." *Journal of Political Economy,* Vol. 71, April 1963, pp. 128-140.

Harris, S. *The Market for College Graduates.* Cambridge, Mass.: Harvard University Press, 1949.

Harrison, B. *Education, Training, and the Urban Ghetto.* Baltimore: John Hopkins University Press, 1972.

Havighurst, R.J. *Aging in America: Implications for Education.* Based on NCOA-Louis Harris & Associates, public opinion study, "The Myth and Reality of Aging in America." Washington, D.C.: National Council on the Aging, Inc., 1976.

Hay, J.E. "How Part-time Work Affects Academic Performance." *Journal of College Placements,* Vol, 29, No. 4, 1969 p. 104.

Henry, J.B. "Part-time Employment and Performance of Freshmen." *Journal of College Student Personnel,* Vol. 8, 1967, pp. 257-260.

Herr, E.L. *Vocational Guidance and Human Development.* Boston, Mass: Houghton-Mifflin, 1974.

Hettich, W. "Consumption Benefits from Education" in *Canadian Higher Education in the Seventies.* Edited by Sylvia Ostry. Economic Council of Canada. Ottawa, Information Canada, 1972.

Hill, C.R. "Capacities, Opportunities, and Educational Investments: The Case of the High School Dropout" (unpublished paper, 1977).

259

Holland, J. "The Use and Evaluation of Interest Inventories," in Esther Diamond (ed.), *Issues of Sex Bias and Sex Fairness in Career Interest Measurement*. Washington, D.C.: NIE, 1975.

Horowitz, M.A. and Hernstadt, I.L. *A Study of the Training of Tool and Die Makers*. Boston: Northeastern University, 1969.

Houle, C. "The Changing Goals of Education in the Perspective of Lifelong Learning." *International Review of Education*. Special Number: Lifelong Education and Learning Strategies. Hamburg: UNESCO Institute for Education, 1974.

Huffman, W.E. "Decision Making: The Role of Education," *American Journal of Agricultural Economics*, Vol. 56, No. 1, February 1974, pp. 85-97.

Hyman, H. H., et al. *The Enduring Effects of Education*. Chicago: University of Chicago Press, 1975.

Jencks, C., et al. *Inequality: A Reassessment of the Effect of Family and Schooling in America*. New York: Basic Books, Inc., 1972.

Johnstone, J. W. C. *The Family and Delinquency: A Reappriasal*. Chicago: Institute for Juvenile Research, 1976 (unpublished).

Kalachek, E.D. *The Youth Labor Market*, Policy Papers in Human Resources and Industrial Relations, No. 12. Ann Arbor, Mich.: Institute of Labor and Industrial Relations, University of Michigan-Wayne State University, 1969.

Kelley, S. C., Chirikos, T. N., and Finn, M. *Manpower Forecasting in the United States: An Evaluation of the State of the Art*. Columbus, Ohio: Center for Human Resource Research, The Ohio State University, 1975.

Kerr, C. "The Balkanization of Labor Markets" in *Labor Mobility and Economic Opportunity*, by E. Wight Bakke and others, Cambridge, Mass.: Technology Press of MIT and Wiley, 1954.

Kirchner, E. P. and Vondracek, S. I. "What Do You Want To Be When You Grow Up?" Paper presented at the Annual Convention of the Society for Research in Child Development, Philadelphia, Pa., 1973.

Kohen, A.I., and associates. *Career Thresholds, Vol. 6*, Columbus, Ohio: Center for Human Resources Research, The Ohio State University, 1977.

Kohen, A.I. and Parnes, H.S. "Occupational Information and Labor Market Status: The Case of Young Men," *Journal of*

Human Resources, 10 (Winter 1975), pp. 45-55.

Kohen, A.I. and Breinich, S.C. "Knowledge of the World of Work: A Test of Occupational Information for Young Men." *Journal of Vocational Behavior,* Vol. 6, 1975, pp. 133-144.

Kreps, J.M. "Some Time Dimensions of Manpower Policy," in Eli Ginzberg (ed.), *Jobs for Americans.* New York: Prentice-Hall, 1976.

Kurland, N.D. (ed.) *Entitlement Papers,* NIE Papers in Education and Work: No. 4. Washington, D.C.: The National Institute of Education, 1976.

Layard, R. and Psacharopoulos, G. "The Screening Hypothesis and the Returns to Education." *Journal of Political Economy,* Vol. 82, No. 5, September/October 1974, pp. 985-998.

Lecht, L.A., Matland, M., and Rosen, R. *Changes in Occupational Characteristics Planning Ahead for the 1980's.* New York: The Conference Board, 1976.

Leinhardt, G. "Applying a Classroom Process Model to Instructional Evaluation." Paper presented at Annual Meeting of American Educational Research Association, New York: April 1977 (unpublished).

Lenning, O. T., Munday, L. A., Johnson, O.B., VanderWell, A.R., and Brue, E.J. *Nonintellective Correlates of Grades, Persistence, and Academic Learning in College: The Published Literature Through the Decade of the Sixties.* Monograph 14. Iowa City: ACT, 1974.

Lerner, J., Bergstrom, F., and Champagne, J.E. *Equal Vocational Education.* Report prepared for the Division of Occupational Research and Development, Texas Education Agency. Houston: Center for Human Resources, University of Houston, 1976.

Levin, H.M. "Is a College Education Worth It?" Paper presented, 60th Annual Meeting of ACE, October 12-14, 1977 (preliminary draft, August 1977).

Levine, H. "Strategies for the Application of Foreign Legislation on Paid Educational Leave to the United States Scene." National Institute of Education paper C-74-0107.

Levitan, S.A. and Johnston, B.H. *The Job Corps: A Social Experiment That Works.* Baltimore Md.: John Hopkins University Press, 1975.

Lipton, D., Martinson, R., and Wilkes, J. *The Effectiveness of Correctional Treatment*, A Survey of Treatment Evaluation Studies, New York: 1975.

Lusterman, S. *Education in Industry*. A Research Report from The Conference Board's Public Affairs Research Division, New York: The Conference Board, 1977.

Lusterman, S. "Education for Work: Business Views and Company Program," *The Conference Board Record*, Vol. XIII, No. 5, May 1976, 39-44.

MacGregor, A. "Part-time Work — Good or Bad?" *Journal of College Placement*, Vol. 26, No. 3, 1966, pp. 127-132.

Mangum, G.L. *Employability, Employment, and Income: A Reassessment of Manpower Policy*. Salt Lake City: Olumpus Publishing Co., 1976.

Mangum, G. and Walsh, J. *A Decade of Manpower Development and Training*. Salt Lake City, Utah: Olumpus Publishing Co., 1973.

Marland, S. "Marland on Career Education." *American Education*, Vol. 7, No. 9, November 1971, pp. 25-28.

Maurizi, A. "Occupational Licensing and the Public Interest." *Journal of Political Economy*, Vol. 82, March 1974, pp. 399-413.

McHale, J. World Facts and Trends," *Futures*, Vol. 3, No. 3, September 1971, p. 260.

McKinnon, B.E., Even, B.B., Newlon, B.J., Jerome, D.R., and Syers, V. *Career Guidance Strategies in Arizona*. Phoenix, Az.: Arizona State Department of Education, 1975.

Michael, R.T. "Education and Consumption." In *Education, Income, and Human Behavior*, New York: McGraw-Hill, 1975, pp. 235-252.

Michael, R.T. *The Effect of Education on Efficiency in Consumption*. New York: National Bureau of Economic Research, 1972.

Mincer, J. and Polachek, S. "Family Investments in Human Capital: Earnings of Women," *Journal of Political Economy*, Vol. 82, No. 2, Supplement, March/April 1974, pp. 2-26.

Morris, J. "Some Simple Tests of the Direct Effect of Education on Preference and on Nonmarket Productivity." *Review of Economics and Statistics*, February 1976.

Mott, F.L. and Moore, S.F. "The Determinants and Consequences of Occupational Information for Young Women." Columbus, Ohio: Center for Human Resource Research, The Ohio State University, April 1976.

Mueller, M.W. "Economic Determinants of Volunteer Work by Women," *Signs*, Fol. 1, No. 2, Winter 1975, pp. 325-334.

National Committee on Employment of Youth. *The Transition from School to Work: A Study of Laws, Regulations and Practices Restricting Work Experience and Employment Opportunities for Youth.* New York: Author, June 1975.

National Education Association. *Teacher Supply and Demand in Public Schools*, 1973. Research Division Report. Washington, D.C.: National Education Association, 1974.

National Education Association. "Teacher Supply and Demand in Public Schools, 1975." NEA Research Memo 1976-2, June 1976.

National Education Association Task Force on Under-Utilization of Professional Personnel. *A Critical National Problem: Under-Utilization of Teachers and Other Trained Personnel.* Washington, D.C.: NEA, February 1972.

National Science Foundation. *Federal Funds for Research, Development, and Other Scientific Activities.* Fiscal Years 1975, 1976, and 1977. Vol. XXV, GPO: Washington, D.C. 1976.

Nolan, J.J. *The Effectiveness of the Self-Directed Search Compared with Group Counseling in Promoting Information-seeking Behavior and Realism of Vocational Choice.* Unpublished doctoral dissertation, University of Maryland, 1973.

Okun, A.M. "The Great Stagflation Swamp." *Brookings Bulletin*, Vol 14(3), Fall 1977, pp. 1-7.

Olson, D.R. and Bruner, J.S. "Learning Through Experience and Learning Through Media," Chapter VI in *Media and Symbols: The Forms of Expression, Communication, and Education*, Part I. Chicago: National Society for the Study of Education, 1974.

Olympus Research Corporation. *An Assessment of Vocational Education Programs for the Handicapped Under Part B of the 1968 Amendments to the Vocational Education Act.* Final Report. Salt Lake City, Utah: Author, 1974.

Olympus Research Corporation. *The Total Impact of Manpower Programs: A Four-City Case Study.* Vol. 1 — Summary of the Final Report. Report MEL 71-05, Prepared for the Office of Policy, Evaluation, and Research, ETA/DOL Washington,

D.C.: Author, 1971.

O'Meara, R. *Combating Knowledge Obsolescence II. Employer Tuition-Aid Plans.* New York: National Industrial Conference Board, 1970.

Organization for Economic Co-operation and Development. Through a Task Force chaired by Clark Kerr. *Education and Working Life in Modern Society,* Paris: OECD, 1975.

Perry, C.R. and others. *The Impact of Government Manpower Programs: In General, and on Minorities and Women.* No. 4, Manpower and Human Resources Studies. Philadelphia, Pa.: University of Pennsylvania. the Wharton School, Industrial Relations Unit, 1975.

Personick, V.A. and Sylvester, R.A. "Evaluation of BLS 1970 Economic and Employment Projections," *Monthly Labor Review,* Vol. 99, No. 8, August 1976, pp. 13-26.

Peterson, R.E. and others. *Toward Lifelong Learning in America: A Sourcebook for Planners.* Berkeley, Ca.: ETS, 1978.

Pfeffer, J. "Some Evidence on Occupational Licensing and Occupational Incomes." *Social Forces,* Vol. 53, September 1974, pp. 102-111.

Prediger, D.J., Roth, J.D., and Noeth, R.J. "Career Development of Youth: A Nationwide Study." *Personnel and Guidance Journal,* Vol. 53, No. 2, October 1974, pp. 97-104.

Prescott, E.C. and Cooley, T.F. *Evaluating the Impact of MDTA Programs on Earnings Under Varying Labor Market Conditions.* Final Report MEL 73-09. Philadelphia, Pa.: University of Pennsylvania, October 1972.

Psacharopoulos, G. *Returns to Education: An International Comparison.* Assisted by Keith Hinchliffe. San Francisco, Ca.: Jossey-Bass, 1973.

Ragan, J.F., Jr. "Minimum Wages and the Youth Labor Market." *The Review of Economics and Statistics,* Vol. LIX, No. 2, May 1977, pp. 129-136.

Redmond, R.E. *Increasing Vocational Information Seeking Behaviors of High School Students.* Unpublished doctoral dissertation, University of Maryland, 1972.

Rehn, G. "For Greater Flexibility of Working Life." *OECD Observer,* No. 886. January 1973.

Reubens, B.G. "Vocational Education for All in High School?," Chapter 13 in *Work and the Quality of Life: Resource Papers for Work in America*, James O'Toole (ed.). Cambridge, Mass.: the MIT Press, 1974a.

Reubens, B.G. "Vocational Education: Performance and Potential," *Manpower*, Vol. 6, No. 7, 1974b.

Robin, G.D. *An Assessment of the In-School Neighborhood Youth Corps Projects in Cincinnati and Detroit with Special Reference to Summer-Only and Year-Round Enrollees — Final Report*. Philadelphia, Pa.: National Analysts, Inc., 1969.

Roe, A. *The Psychology of Occupations*. New York: Wiley, 1956.

Schultz, T.W. "The Value of the Ability to Deal with Disequilibria." *Journal of Economic Literature*. Vol. 13, No. 3, September 1975, pp. 827-846.

Secretary General's Ad Hoc Group on the Relations Between Education and Employment. *Education and Working Life in Modern Society*. Paris: OECD, 1975.

Semas, P.W. "Production of Teachers Drops by 6.2 Percent." *Chronicle of Higher Education*, July 11, 1977, p. 7.

Sewell, D.O. *Training the Poor*. Kingston, Ontario: Industrial Relations Center, Queen's University, 1971.

Shaeffer, R.G. "College Recruiting in 1976 and the Prospects for Future Graduates." *The Conference Board Record*, Vol. XIII, No. 3, March 1976, pp. 46-52.

Shaeffer, R.G. "The Buyers' Market for New College Grads." *The Conference Board Record*, Vol. XII, No. 2, February 1975, pp. 45-51.

Shimberg, B. *Improving Occupational Regulations: Officials from 30 States Discuss Common Problems and Search for Solutions*. Final Report to Employment and Training Administration, U.S. Department of Labor, under Grant No. 21-34-75-12. Princeton, N.J.: Educational Testing Service, 1976.

Shimberg, B. and others. *Occupational Licensing: Practices and Policies*. Washington, D.C.: Public Affairs Press, 1973.

Smith, D.H. "Research and Communication Needs in Voluntary Action," Chapter 7 in J.G. Cull & R.E. Hardy (eds.). *Volunteerism: An Emerging Profession*. Springfield, Ill.: Charles C. Thomas, Publishers, 1974.

265

Smith, J.P. and Welch, F.R. "Black-White Male Wage Ratios: 1960-70." *The American Economic Review*, Vol. 67, No. 3, June 1977, pp. 323-338.

Somers, G.G. and Stromsdorfer, E.W. *A Cost Effectiveness Study of the In-School and Summer Neighborhood Youth Corps.* Madison, Wi.: Industrial Relations Research Institute, University of Wisconsin, 1970.

Sommers, D. and Eck, A. "Occupational Mobility in the American Labor Force." *Monthly Labor Review*, Vol. 100, No. 1, January 1977, pp. 3-19.

Stern, B.E. "Application of Information Systems to Career and Job Choice," in S.L. Wolfbein (ed.), *Labor Market Information for Youths*. Philadelphia, Pa.: School of Business Administration, Temple University, 1975.

Stoner, J.A.F., Ference, T.P., Warren, E.K., and Christensen, H.K. "Patterns and Plateaus in Managerial Careers — An Exploratory Study,' Research Paper No. 66, Columbia University, Graduate School of Business, August 1974.

Stromsdorfer, E.W. *Review and Synthesis of Cost-Effectiveness Studies of Vocational and Technical Education.* Information Series No. 57. Columbus, Ohio: ERIC Clearinghouse, Center for Vocational and Technical Education, The Ohio State University, August 1972.

Stromsdorfer, E.W. *An Economic Analysis of the Work Experience and Career Exploration Program: 1971-72 School Year.* Final Report to the Manpower Administration, Department of Labor, July 1973.

Stromsdorfer, E.W. *An Economic and Institutional Analysis of the Co-operative Vocational Education Program in Dayton, Ohio.* Washington, D.C. U.S. Department of Commerce, National Technical Information Service, 1973a.

Super, D.E. *The Psychology of Careers*. New York: Harper and Row, 1957.

Swerdloff, S. "How Good Were Manpower Projections for the 1960s," *Monthly Labor Review*, Vol. 92, No. 11, November 1969, pp. 17-22.

Taubman, P. "Earnings, Education, Genetics, and Environment," *The Journal of Human Resources*, Vol. XI, No. 4, Fall 1976, pp. 447-461.

266

Taubman, P. and Wales, T. "Higher Education, Mental Ability, and Screening," *Journal of Political Economy*, Vol. 81, No. 1, January-February 1973, pp. 28-56.

Thorndike, R.T. and Hagen, E. *Characteristics of Men Who Remained In and Left Teaching.* Cooperative Research Project No. 574 (SAE8189) of the U.S. Office of Education. New York: Teachers College, Columbia University, 1959.

Thurow, L.C. *Generating Inequality: Mechanisms of Distribution in the U.S. Economy.* New York: Basic Books, Inc., 1975.

Thurow, L.C. "Measuring the Economic Benefits of Education," in M.S. Gordon (ed.), *Higher Education and the Labor Market.* New York: McGraw-Hill, 1974.

Thurow, L.C. *Poverty and Discrimination.* Washington, D.C.: The Brookings Institute, 1969.

Tillery, D. *Distribution and Differentiation of Youth: A Study of Transition from School to College.* Cambridge, Mass.: Ballinger Publishing Co., 1973.

Trueblood, D.L. "Effects of Employment on Academic Achievement." *Personnel and Guidance Journal*, Vol. 36, 1957, pp. 112-115.

U.S. Bureau of Labor Statistics. *Handbook of Labor Statistics 1975: Reference Edition*, Washington, D.C.: GPO, 1975.

U.S. Bureau of Labor Statistics. *Occupational Projections and Training Data.* Bulletin 1918. Washington, D.C.: GPO, 1976.

U.S. Bureau of Labor Statistics. *Youth Unemployment and Minimum Wages.* Bulletin 1657. Washington, D.C.: GPO, 1970.

U.S. Congressional Budget Office. *Budget Options for the Youth Employment Problems*, Background Paper No. 20. Washington, D.C.: GPO, March 1977.

U.S. Congressional Budget Office. *Public Employment and Training Assistance: Alternative Federal Approaches*, Budget Issue Paper. Washington, D.C.: GPO, February 1977.

U.S. Department of Health, Education, and Welfare. *Indicators of Educational Outcomes: Fall 1972.* Washington, D.C.: GPO, 1973.

U.S. Department of Labor, Manpower Administration. *Occupational Licensing and the Supply of Nonprofessional Manpower.* Manpower Research Monograph No. 11. Washington, D.C.: GPO, 1969.

U.S. Department of Labor, Manpower Administration. *Women in Apprenticeship — Why Not?* Manpower Research Monograph No. 33. Washington, D.C.: GPO, 1974.

U.S. Department of Labor. *Manpower Report of the President.* Washington, D.C.: GPO, 1975.

U.S. General Accounting Office. *Career Education: Status and Needed Improvements.* MWD-76-81. Washington, D.C.: Author, January 26, 1976.

U.S. Office of Management and Budget. *The United States Budget in Brief.* Fiscal Year 1979, GPO: Washington, D.C., 1978, pp. 76-81.

U.S. National Center for Education Statistics. *Projections of Education Statistics to 1985-86.* Washington, D.C. GPO, 1977.

U.S. National Center for Education Statistics. *Digest of Education Statistics, 1975 Edition.* Washington, D.C.: GPO, 1976.

U.S. President. *Employment and Training of the President.* Washington, D.C.: GPO, 1977.

Vincent, H. "An Analysis of Vocational Education in Our Secondary Schools." Washington, D.C.: Office of Program Planning and Evaluation, U.S. Office of Education, July 1969 (revised).

Von Moltke, K. and Schneevoight, N. *Educational Leaves for Employees: European Experience for American Consideration.* A Report for the Carnegie Council on Policy Studies in Higher Education. San Francisco: Jossey-Bass Publishers, 1976.

Wachter, M.L. "Primary and Secondary Labor Markets: A Critique of the Dual Approach," in *Brookings Papers on Economic Activity*, 3, 1974.

Walsh, J. and Totten, J. *An Assessment of Vocational Education Programs for the Disadvantaged Under Part B and Part A Sec. 102(b) of the 1968 Amendments to the Vocational Education Act. Final Report.* Salt Lake City, Utah Olympus Research Centers, December 1976.

Walther, R. and Magnusson, M. *Neighborhood Youth Corps: A Review of Research*, Manpower Research Monograph 13, GPO, Washington, D.C.: 1970.

Warmbrod, J.R. *Review and Synthesis of Research on the Economics of Vocational Education*, Research 16. Columbus, Ohio: Center for Vocational and Technical Education, The Ohio State University, November 1968.

Watkins, B. "Certification of Professionals: A Bonanza for Extension Programs," *The Chronicle of Higher Education*, April 11, 1977, p. 8.

Weaver, W.Y. "Educators in Supply and Demand: Effects on Quality." Prepared for the Annual Meeting of the American Education Research Association. April 6, 1977.

Weaver, W.T. "Educators in Supply and Demand: Effects on Quality," *School Review*, Vol. 86, No. 8 (August 1978).

Weisbrod, B.A. *External Benefits of Public Education: An Economic Analysis.* Princeton, N.J.: Industrial Relations Section, Department of Economics, Princeton University, 1964.

Welch, F. "Minimum-Wage Legislation in the United States" in *Evaluating the Labor-Market Effects of Social Programs*, Orley-Ashenfelter and James Blum (ed.), Princeton, N.J.: Princeton University, Industrial Relations Section, 1976, pp. 1-38.

Wicker, T. *New York Times.* April 25, 1975.

Wiley, D.E. and Harnischfeger, A. "Statement to the House Committee on Education and Labor, Subcommittee on Elementary, Secondary, and Vocational Education," May 11, 1977 (unpublished).

Wilson, J.W. and Lyons, E.H. *Work-Study College Programs.* New York: Harper and Brothers, 1961.

Wilson, S.R. and Wise, L.L. *The American Citizen: 11 Years After High School.* Vol. 1, Palo Alto: American Institutes for Research/Project Talent, 1975.

Wirtz, W. and the National Manpower Institute. *The Boundless Resource: A Prospectus for an Education-Work Policy.* Washington, D.C.: The New Republic Book Co., Inc., 1975.

Wool, H. *The Labor Supply for Lower Level Occupations.* Research and Development Monograph 42, U.S. Department of Labor, Employment and Training Administration, Washington, D.C.: GPO, 1976.

Yencso, W.R. "Comparing Engineering Graduates from Cooperative and Regular Programs." *Engineering Education*, Vol. 61, April 1971, pp. 816-818.

Young, A.M. "Going Back to School at 35 and Over," *Monthly Labor Review*, Vol. 100, No. 7, July 1977, pp. 43-45.

269

Young, R.C. *Manpower Demand: Information Guidelines for Educational, Vocational Education, and Manpower Planning.* Columbus, Ohio: Center for Vocational and Technical Education, The Ohio State University, 1973.

Zaccaria, J. *Theories of Occupational Choice and Vocational Development.* Boston, Mass.: Houghton Mifflen, 1970.

Zener, T. and Schnuelle, L. *An Evaluation of the Self-Directed Search: A Guide to Educational and Occupational Planning.* Report 124. Baltimore, Md.: Center for the Social Organization of Schools, Johns Hopkins University, 1972.

Index

Adams, F.C., 91
Allen, B.V., 112
Andrisani, P.J., 60
Arbeiter, S., 112
Arrow, K., 10
Ashenfelter, O., 149, 151
Augsburger, J.D., 91, 92

Bachman, J.G., 155
Baker, H.B., 92
Bakke, E. Wight, 248
Barton, Paul, 154, 160, 198
Baytos, 250
Becker, G.S., 64, 134
Benham, L., 167
Berg, I., 9, 64, 71
Best, F., 122, 125
Bird, C., 9, 71, 85
Bisconti, A.S., 69
Borus, Michael, E., 58, 89
153, 250
Bowen, Howard R., 66
Bowles, E., 135, 136
Bowlsbey, J.A.N., 114, 115
Breneman, David W., 39, 40,
245, 246
Brennan, J.P., 89, 153
Bruner, J.S. 76
Budd, W.C., 92
Burkhardt, C., 121

Cain, C.G., 60, 246
Cairnes, J.E., 8
Campbell, A., 68, 69
Campbell, David, 117
Campbell, R.E., 110
Carey, M.L., 26, 28
Carlson, R.J., 164
Carter, Jimmy, 144, 181
Cartter, Allan, 29
Chrysler, E., 165
Cicourel, A.V., 117
Cole, N.S., 111
Coleman, J.S., 14, 43, 67, 84
Converse, P.E., 68
Cooley, T.F., 149, 151, 152,
157
Cremin, L.A., 67
Crites, J.O., 111
Cross, K.P., 95

Denison, E.F., 72
Diamond, Esther, 111
Doeringer, P.B., 8, 59
Drewes, D.W., 37, 46
Dunlop, J.T., 8, 248
Dunn, K., 121
Dunn, P., 121

Eck, A., 38
Eckaus, R., 65
Edelstein, 250

Ehrenberg, R.G., 156
Elliott, D., 155
Enderlein, T.E., 118
Endicott, Frank S., 34, 46

Farber, D., 149
Faulk, D.C., 58
Feldstein, M., 57
Fine, B., 75
Finn, 245
Flaim, P.D., 25
Fowler, Charles, 85
Freedman, M., 161
Freeman, Richard B., 31, 39
40, 53, 65, 66, 189, 245, 246
Freschi, 250
Friedman, N., 93, 95
Froomkin, J., 125, 126, 129
Fuchs, V.R., 66
Fullerton, H.N., Jr., 25

Ganley, John, 97
Ginzberg, Eli, 106, 107, 134,
219, 220, 226-229, 244
Glenny, 250
Glover, R.W., 80
Goldstein, J.H., 153, 155
Gomberg, William, 246, 247
Gordon, D.M., 59
Gordon, Margaret, 4, 31, 82
Gordon, R.A., 198
Gore, G., 95
Gramlich, E.M., 56
Grandy, T.G., 108
Grasso, J.T., 78-81, 85
Griliches, Z., 97, 98

Hagen, E., 107
Hanoch, G., 65
Hansen, W.L., 64, 246
Hanson, G.R., 111
Harbison, 248

Harnischfeger, A., 12, 13,
72-74
Harris, Seymour, 40
Harrison, Bennett, 59
Havighurst, R.J., 69
Hawes, 249
Hay, J.E., 92, 104
Henry, J.B. 92
Hernstadt, I.L., 80
Herr, E.L., 108
Hettich, W., 66
Hewlett, J.G., 156
Hill, C.R., 198
Hill, Russell, 119
Holland, J., 108, 118
Horowitz, M.A., 80
Houle, Cyril, 139
Huffman, W.E., 68
Humphrey, Hubert, 143
Hyman, H.H., 69

Jencks, C., 9, 14, 43, 63,
67, 84
Johnson, Lyndon, 46
Johnston, B.H., 153
Johnstone, J.W.C., 67

Kalachek, E.D., 53, 57, 58
Katz, D.S., 37, 46
Kelley, S.C., 36
Kerr, Clark, 8, 59, 219, 248
Kiefer, 149
Kirchner, E.P., 108
Kitsuse, J.I., 117
Kleiner, 162
Knowles, B., 155
Kohen, A.I., 72, 119
Kreplin, 250
Kreps, J.M., 123
Kurland, N.D., 139

Layard, R., 11, 72

Lecht, L.A., 46
Leinhardt, G., 74
Lenning, Oscar, 92
Lerner, J. 113
Levine, H., 137
Levitan, S.A., 153
Lipton, D., 155
Lusterman, S., 126, 179
Lyons, E.H., 95

MacGregor, A., 92
McGuire, T.W., 149, 151, 152
McHale, J., 123
McKinnon, B.E., 109
Magnusson, M., 154
Malfetti, 251
Mangum, G.L., 148, 149, 237
Marland, Sidney, 63, 113
Marshall, R., 80
Martinson, R., 155
Matland, M., 46
Maurizi, A., 163
Medsker, 250
Michael, R.T., 67, 68
Mincer, J., 139
Moore, S.F., 119
Morris, J., 67
Mott, F.L., 119
Mueller, M.W., 134, 139
Myers, 248

Nixon, Richard, 143
Noeth, R.J., 110, 117
Nolan, J.J., 118
Nyquist, Ewald B., 248-249

Okun, A.M., 198
Olson, D.R., 76
O'Meara, R., 136

Parnes, Herbert, 58, 60, 72
75, 97, 119

Perry, C.R., 89, 148, 152, 153
Personick, V.A., 36
Pfeffer, J., 163
Phillips, Louis, 164
Piore, M.J., 59
Polachek, S., 139
Prediger, D.J., 110, 117
Prescott, E.C., 149, 151, 152
Psacharopoulos, G., 11, 71, 72

Ragan, J.F., Jr., 57
Redmond, R.E., 118
Reed, J.S., 69
Rehn, G., 123
Reubens, B.G., 78
Robin, G.D., 89, 154, 226,
Rodgers, W.L., 68
Roe, A., 107
Rosen, R., 46
Rosen, S., 89, 153
Roth, J.D., 110, 117
Royer, 250
Ruch, F., 251
Ruyle, 250

Schaeffer, 34
Schnuelle, L., 118
Schultz, Theodore, 68
Sewell, D.O., 152
Shaeffer, R.G., 34
Shea, John R., 78, 80, 81, 85
249, 250
Shimberg, B., 163
Shostak, 247
Smith, D.H., 139
Snider, Patricia, 250
Somers, G.G., 89
Sommers, D., 38
Stephens, C.W., 91
Stern, B., 115, 122, 125
Stromsdorfer, E.W., 54, 78
89, 90, 226

273

Super, D.E., 107
Swerdloff, S., 36
Sylvester, R.A., 36

Taubman, P., 64, 71
Thorndike, R.T., 107
Thurow, L.C., 32, 123, 198
Tillery, D., 106
Totten, J., 90
Trueblood, D.L., 92

Vincent, Howard, 79
Von Moltke, K., 137
Vondracek, S.I., 108

Wachter, M.L., 59
Wales, T., 64
Walsh, J., 90, 148
Walther, R., 154
Warmbrod, J.R., 78
Watkins, B., 165
Weaver, W., 43, 47
Weisbrod, B.A., 66
Welch, F., 56
Wicker, Tom, 160
Wiley, D.E., 12, 13, 72-74
Wilkes, J., 155
Williams, E. Belvin, 251
Wilson, J.W., 95
Wilson, S.R., 70
Wirtz, Willard, 12, 13, 54, 74,
219, 222, 223, 225-228
Wise, L.L., 70
Wolfson, R.J., 125, 126, 129
Wool, H., 31
Wright, C.R., 69

Yencso, W.R., 95
Young, A.M., 6
Young, R.C., 37

Zaccaria, J., 107

Zener, T., 118
Zytowski, Donald, 121